God of the Weak Things

H. Bryan Allen

God of the Weak Things

H. Bryan Allen

Parson's Porch Books

God of the Weak Things

Copyright © 2012 by H. Bryan Allen

ISBN: 978-1-936912-60-5   Softcover

All rights reserved. No part of this book may be reproduced or transmitted in any form or by any means, electronic or mechanical, including photocopying, recording, or by any information storage and retrieval system, without permission in writing from the publisher.

This book was printed in the United States of America.

To order additional copies of this book, contact:

Parson's Porch & Company

1-423-475-7308

www.parsonsporchbooks.com

TABLE OF CONTENTS

PREFACE	7
ACKNOWLEDGEMENTS	9
FOREWORD	11
Introduction	15
Just a Little In the Hands of God	19
Heart to Heart	24
The Wooing Power of Our Weaknesses	31
Thunder and Lightning	36
Extra Mile Parenting	57
The Call of Sister	71
The Call of Brother	79
The Call of Work	87
The Call of Pain: The Helping Hurt	101
When God and Weakness Merge: Jesus	108

FOREWORD

(Jesus said) "…My grace is sufficient for thee: for my strength is made perfect in weakness.

(The Apostle Paul concluded): Most gladly therefore will I rather glory in my infirmities that the power of Christ may rest upon me.

…when I am weak, then I am strong."

(II Corinthians 12: 9, 10b) KJV

"But God hath chosen the foolish things of the world to confound the wise; and God hath chosen the weak things of the world to confound the things that are mighty."

(I Corinthians 1:1) KJV

Preface

Simply stated, Bryan Allen is a family man, a working man and a pastor. I am just an ordinary guy who has been immensely blessed to accomplish extraordinary things while housed in a very unorthodox body. The effects of being born with multiple, congenital birth defects afforded me a very bleak prognosis for what little life span was expected. However, I chose to use these seemingly dismal "defects" to achieve some God-glorifying effects! Now at age 53, God continues to empower my initially pronounced disadvantages to His advantage by helping others to embrace both their strengths and weaknesses. In so doing, I am blessed to lead others to a saving knowledge of Jesus Christ while simultaneously helping them to know that God yearns to use all that they are and all that they are about in order to fulfill His grand plan for them. Not only does God use our strengths but to no lesser degree, He in His sovereignty and omnipotence uses our weaknesses as the often overlooked and untapped gems we possess.

God is good and so is life! I earned a B.S.B.A from Kennesaw College and a M. Div. from New Orleans Baptist Theological Seminary. I currently reside in rural Alabama in the town of

Duncanville with my precious wife and our youngest son. Our oldest son lives in nearby Tuscaloosa (ROLL TIDE!). I am in my 34th year as a minister of the Gospel of Jesus Christ. I am in my 25th year as the System Safety Consultant of a rural water system. I have pastored three churches over a span of 24 years. I also ministered through vocational evangelism for two years. I currently serve voluntarily as an Associate Pastor of a nearby church. The Lord willing, I hope to pastor a church for the Lord again someday.

I pray that this book will be a blessing to all who read it.

Pastor Bryan

ACKNOWLEDGEMENTS

First and foremost, Jesus Christ is my personal Lord and Savior. He is the only way I can raise my head from the pillow every day. I give Him all the praise, honor and glory because from Him all blessings flow. He has been with me every step of every day. He is always faithful and true. He never changes and His compassions fail not!

Second, my wife and Princess Angel, Renee, is second only to Jesus Himself in my life. She is my most treasured critic. Her candid honesty has challenged me to prayerfully examine many issues as I never would have otherwise. From the moment we first met, she has loved me from my heart and outward from there. By this, I mean she has patiently loved the unique challenges presented by my physical differences/weaknesses. I guess this can be best expressed by a statement she shared with my sister long ago. Renee declared: "When I hold Bryan's finger on his left arm, I'm holding his hand, not a finger or a deformity." This statement echoes the approach of her devotion, dedication and love for me throughout the years. I am so glad I waited on God to provide her as my wife!

Third, my two sons stir me on to greater heights. Ben (Thunder) and Zach (Lightning) are my dreams fulfilled. I have watched them play the sports I was never able to play. I have shared in the joys and heartaches of their first cars (trucks actually) and the eventual totaling of each! I have navigated the "tugboat" (of sorts) alongside them as they have travelled through the seas of romance. Now, I am beginning to enjoy their entry into manhood. The kindred spirit I enjoy with them is a priceless treasure only God can provide.

Billy and Betty Allen are my precious parents who never gave up on me. They will always be held in my heart as the dual foundations of all that I am or ever hope to become. They loved me just the right way. They protected me just enough but allowed me to take the necessary blows and falls to instill in me the resolve to never quit. Their sixty years of devoted marriage provide for me an eternal example for my own marriage. Most of all, they taught me to put Jesus first. Due to that lesson, I know I will be with them again in heaven where they await my arrival.

My sister Diann Dilbeck is the one who first stirred me to serious consideration of my need for salvation. I treasure the close relationship we share. Most people declare that she and I speak our own alien language to each other! We will always be kids at heart! I would not have it any other way. Diann's watch-care over our parents proved instrumental in my being able to obediently leave home long ago in order to answer God's call into the Gospel ministry. She will have many jewels in her crown as her share in the souls I have been privileged to lead to Jesus.

My special friend and brother Bill Odom has always been that friend and companion we all need. He has been brutally honest with my various "performances" over the years and admittedly, I have been the same in return toward him. Together, we have been to life's mountaintops as well as to hell's gates a time or two! He is exemplary in what Christ commanded of us when it comes to selfless service. In so doing, countless others and I have benefitted eternally.

The three churches I have been privileged to pastor have afforded to me an immeasurable wealth of life's best and fullest living. Valley Head Baptist Church, Cornelius Chapel Baptist Church, and Akron Baptist Church all looked beyond what is on the outside and allowed me to fully apply my heart as their pastor. No words or combination of words are adequate to express my gratitude to them.

The members of my wife's family have been instruments of various strengths over the years. They are not my in-laws but rather, they are my family too. They have loved me likewise and for this, I am both humbled and blessed beyond words.

In closing, the heroes of the Christian faith that served as my professors at New Orleans Baptist Theological Seminary made an indelible impression on my life. Particularly, my Preaching Professor, Dr. Harold Bryson, proved to be a major catalyst for writing this book. My Evangelism Professor, Dr. Cecil Randall, befriended Renee and me in the years following my graduation. His compassion and zeal for souls ignited my commitment to never give up on anybody. Finally, three men who served as my pastors over the course of my life stand as towers of unswerving strength and examples of faith. They are the late Rev. W. R. Simmone, the late Rev. Don Hazel and Dr. Henry Fields.

Upon reflection of all the aforementioned, I share this verse: "I thank my God upon my every remembrance of you." (Philippians 1:3, KJV)

Introduction

This book describes what the Lord of all has enabled me to accomplish despite my frailties. My candor and humor about my physical differences may startle some readers. However, the candor and humor enable others to talk to me openly without focusing on my differences.

Weaknesses and frailties were obviously an inherent part of my body. I was born with multiple, physical, congenital birth defects. Both arms are shorter than usual. Instead of hands, I have only a thumb on my left arm and a "mitten-shaped" appendage on my right arm. (At an early age, my youngest son called it my "chicken nugget"!) On my right leg was a severely deformed "club-foot" containing only four toes. I only have one-half of a left leg, and nothing below the knee. There was a "perfect" foot with five toes immediately at the knee. The awkward angle of this foot made it a constant source of pain for weight-bearing. Therefore, it was amputated when I was six. The lower quarter of my spinal column sways outward which makes my buttocks protrude when I try to stand. I always referred to my rear end as a "cow-catcher" much like those found on the front of steam locomotives! However, being from the south, it is most often referred to as a "butt". My parents never whipped my "buttocks" but rather, my "butt"! To have debated that with them would surely have resulted in extra licks! At any rate, my wife thinks I have a cute butt! "Nuff" said!

As an infant, surgeons tried without success to correct the deformity of my right foot in hopes of providing increased mobility in the years to come. I spent the next fourteen years wearing a very complicated, uncomfortable, and confining four stage brace on my right leg.

This brace was in addition to an artificial prosthesis on my left leg (more commonly referred to as a wooden leg). However, this cumbersome arrangement facilitated my ability to walk my first fourteen years. At age fourteen, a radical, experimental, reconstructive surgery of my right foot was performed. Though the next four months were full of a very painful and grueling process of healing and rehabilitation, the surgery was deemed successful because at last, I was free of the need to wear the brace on my right leg! All that was required was a custom-built shoe. My mobility was maximized at my greatest time of need: high school and college. I only had to use a wheelchair when great distances had to be traversed over short periods of time. During those years, I even enjoyed weight lifting. Physically, those ten years were the best in my life. But as the doctors had cautioned, I began to struggle with the premature wear of my hips and lower back. Now in my fifties, I am physically 90% dependent on a wheelchair. Thus, even while this book is a work in progress, I continue to come to grips with my weaknesses as I trust in God's daily strength.

As I launch into this project, I do so following a year of prayerful consideration as to how I am to tackle such an additional undertaking in light of my current "full plate" in life. I have been serving the past ten and one-half years at my third pastorate. It is bi-vocational. I am in my twenty-forth year with my secular employer. Easter Sunday 2011 was my last Sunday in my latest pastorate. I am at peace that the Lord would have me take a sabbatical from my pastoral ministry in order to write. The year of prayerful struggle preceding this decision endured in its longevity for two reasons: First, third only to my love for the Lord and my family is my love for preaching God's Word. Second, when I enter the pulpit, it is as if the Lord gives me a brief respite from my physical challenges and the weaknesses they impose. The pains and the differences are somehow put on hold for the duration of the preaching moment and God allows me to experience a temporary, physiological freedom. Ironically, it is during these events that I often give focus to my weaknesses in order to exalt God's omnipotence! Yes, He truly does work in strange ways! When one is built as strangely as I, all this just makes sense! Admittedly, my prayers have been mingled with implorations for opportunities to preach whenever possible. In addition, once this writing is complete, I truly hope to pastor again someday. I am willing if the Lord is willing!

Just a Little in the Hands of God

All things are best handled by God's hands. Through God, our greatest achievements are met, our highest hopes come to fruition and our greatest potential is engaged. I am convinced these accomplishments are afforded their maximum development through our weaknesses. Let me explain. When we commend into God's hands the best of our talents and strengths, we fully expect grand results for which we should be grateful. However, our expectations are often unjustifiably less when we commend into God's hands that which is frail, weak and less desirable. Why? Are our weaknesses any less part of us than our strengths? Such reasoning would consider a weaker eye, arm or leg to be a lesser part of our being than their stronger counterpart. Is the power of God's hands lessened by the weak things that are commended unto Him with as much sincerity as our commendation of the strong things? Indeed not! Perhaps just the opposite is the case!

The Bible describes Jesus observing the worshipers as they cast their offerings into the temple treasury. "And He (Jesus) looked up and saw the rich putting their gifts into the treasury, and He saw also a certain, poor widow putting in two mites. So He said, 'Truly

I say to you that this poor widow has put in more than all; for all these out of their abundance have put in offerings for God, but she out of her poverty put in all the livelihood that she had'." (Luke 21:1-4, NKJV) With no intentions of demeaning the larger gifts of those with greater assets, Jesus saw the immense power and faith portrayed by the two mites given by the poor widow. She gave her all. Her all was weak and next to nothing so far as economics were concerned. However, her all in the hands of God even stirred the applause of God Himself! As this widow in all of her poverty cast into God's hands the weak trifle that she did possess, was she concerned that starvation was her certain doom? No, but rather, I am persuaded of her conviction that her all, even if it was next to nothing, would amount to much if given to God!

The widow's plight was as low as it gets in her day. Her image portrayed the very essence of being pitiable and weak. Her actions epitomize what we all should do with all we are and possess. As the widow gave her all, as weak and small as it was, little did she know that her actions would receive God's eternal accolades! Obviously, the "greater" gifts of the masses facilitated and perhaps allowed an increase in temple operations. The widow's gift would soon be mirrored by Jesus Himself as He gave His all at Calvary. Despite all the power and strength afforded to Him by the Heavenly Father along with a full force of ten-thousand legions of angels, Jesus instead obediently chose the weak frailty of a battered, broken, bloody, crucified human frame to eternally save our souls from hell! After so doing, His chosen weakness was transformed by

God's unparalleled resurrection power! Indeed, the weak things entrusted into the hands of God procure our greatest achievements, exceed our highest hopes and fulfills our most desired purpose.

The resurrection of the brutally beaten, dead Son of God was the Almighty's foremost demonstration of what He can do when we place into His hands that which seems utterly defeated and void of all strength! One of my favorite examples of God's ordaining use of the weak and base to show forth His power is recorded in the following scriptures: "…When Jesus heard it (the death of John the Baptist); He departed from there by boat to a deserted place by Himself. But when the multitudes heard it, they followed Him on foot from the cities. And when Jesus went out, He saw a great multitude; and He was moved with compassion for them, and healed their sick. When it was evening, His disciples came to Him saying, 'This is a deserted place, and the hour is already late. Send the multitudes away, that they may go into the villages and buy themselves food.' But Jesus said to them, 'They do not need to go away. You give them something to eat.' And they said to Him, 'We have here only five loaves and two fish.' He said, 'Bring them here to Me.' Then, He commanded the multitudes to sit down on the grass. And He took the five loaves and the two fish, and looking up to heaven, He blessed and broke and gave the loaves to the disciples; and the disciples gave to the multitudes. So they all ate and were filled, and they took up twelve baskets full of the fragments that remained. Now those that had eaten were about five thousand men, besides women and children." (Matthew 14:13-21 NKJV)

Jesus was exhausted from an extenuating period of ministering to the multitudes. Numerous times, He had healed from diseases and delivered from demons, as recorded in the other Gospels. Upon receiving the news of John the Baptist's beheading, Jesus left the crowds to a retreat in a deserted place. All indications were that this was no luxury resort by any stretch of the imagination. Despite its sparse accommodations, this place was temporarily commissioned by Jesus for solace, rest and perhaps even to grieve over His much admired comrade, John the Baptist. This scene in and of itself paints a portrayal of mankind weakened and wearied by life's load. Here, Jesus is briefly found alone. Soon, however, the pursuit of the needful multitudes bombarded this weary hero who had tirelessly released so many of them from their agonies.

Please understand that I am in no wise referring to Jesus as weak. I simply readily acknowledge that He taught us how to live our lives in these bodies of flesh even during those times when we have reached the very edge of our physical and emotional limits. Such extents can tempt us to give up and hide in our tired and weakened state. Despite His best efforts to take a break, Jesus was compelled to meet the needs of people at the expense of ignoring His own. Moved with compassion, Jesus ministered until the day was drawing to a close. Then the disciples reminded Jesus of what He knew all too well. The disciples thought they had a predicament. They and Jesus were now facing this huge crowd of five-thousand men plus their families. Daylight was dwindling and they barely had enough groceries to feed themselves much less this hungry multitude in the desert. The disciples therefore implored Jesus to send the crowd away into the villages to provide themselves food. The disciples focused only upon the weaknesses of their plight. Indeed, their plight would remain hopeless and weak as long as it remained in the hands of man. Then, the weary, resolute Master began to prod His disciples to place their plight into the hands of God. As the disciples again focused on their meager food supply, Jesus definitively tells them to bring the food to Him. Absorb this picture, dear reader: Weak and meager portions were being placed into the hands of a wearied but omnipotent Savior by a group of uncertain disciples for a hopelessly, huge crowd of famished people. Now that the weakness of it all had been placed into God's hands, the "little bit" became a surplus. The desert place was soon shown to have grass for the people to recline upon while they ate! Think of it! Grass in a desert place! Amazing!

At that point, Jesus thanked God for what they had. At that very point, the meager portions were transformed into an abundant surplus! Indeed, in the hands of God, a little bit is a whole lot! Even weak, base things and people placed into the hands of God can, and will, be used by God for an abundance of good! In so doing, God presses it all down, shakes it together and it runs over!

To God be the glory!

Heart to Heart

This chapter and the rest of the book explain how God has highlighted my weaknesses to enhance the strengths of others. A few of the many who have helped me are described. They helped me commit both my strengths and weaknesses to God.

An old adage says that God works in strange ways. Some of His ways have been especially strange in dealing with my weaknesses. Repeatedly, He has adjoined my weaknesses to the strengths of others and in so doing, has increased their strengths in their response to my weaknesses. In no case does this apply more than in the person of my beloved wife Renee.

After earning my Bachelor of Science Degree in Business Administration, I left the comforts and securities of my childhood home at age 23 in December of 1982 to attend graduate school at the New Orleans Baptist Theological Seminary (NOBTS). New Orleans seemed like foreign soil compared to my North Georgia home. Louisiana's state bird should be the mosquito! The sea level difference between the Blue Ridge Mountains and New Orleans is an eternity. Home has four seasons. New Orleans has two seasons: damp with 100% humidity and hot with 200% humidity! The occasional North Georgia roach can be merely trampled underfoot. The frequent Cajun roach can be saddled and ridden! The veins of North Georgia drivers are filled with sweet iced tea. Those in New Orleans bulge with fermented ammonia!

There I was, weaknesses and all, in my efficiency apartment facing all of these radical life changes and worst of all, I was alone. There was no MaMa to prepare my meals and do my laundry—neither of which I had ever done before. I had no microwave…just a toaster oven and a very small gas stove in my kitchenette the age of which gave me visions of pyrotechnic chaos if I were to ignite it! Gone were the securities of my Dad who had access to solving any problem that may arise. The closeness that had developed between my sister and me was over 500 miles away. "Homesick" soon became the challenge that made all the challenges of physical weaknesses pale in comparison. "Homesick" and all that goes with it was new turf to say the least. Granted, I had developed a lot of grit during my first 23 years of overcoming. Now, all I had was Jesus. His omnipotence sustained me through the new experience of living life solo. The idea of learning to swim by someone throwing you into the water took on new meaning.

I soon learned the blessedness of bologna sandwiches, TV dinners and canned foods. I became vividly acquainted with the campus clothes "washeteria". Even though the campus was a Southern Baptist Seminary, this "washeteria" was from the depths of Sheol (place of shadowy existence in the Hebrew)!

The washers only worked on one of two cycles: cold and heavy or hot and heavy. The dryers had only one setting: burnt! Thankfully, I had received a hand-held clothes steamer that removed some of the prune effect out of my clothes. Tackling all of the aforementioned, working at the campus post office and maintaining my classwork kept me busy indeed. However, I was still immensely homesick and so very lonely.

I never moved to New Orleans to find a wife. I just wanted to get in and out ASAP! I had dated a couple of young ladies before leaving Georgia. Marriage talk even entered the picture. However, that soon ended when the word "preacher" came into focus. This calling of God upon my life soon proved to be a lifesaver. My third month at seminary, I was in the daily chapel service. There, I was introduced to Renee. My heart almost stopped! Her smile and her eyes grabbed my heart from the start. Neither of us had a second period class, so every class day between first and third class, we talked in the hallway about so many things. During the third week of our hall chats, I asked her out on a date---and she said YES!! Oh glorious day!! Homesick?!?! Who?!?! Me?!?! Perish the thought!!

Our first date was at Chuck-E-Cheese Pizza. We both worked part-time campus jobs for minimum wage so this date was indeed a splurge! But it was worth it! Many of our successive dates cost little or nothing at all. Some were spent picnicking at City Park. Others were comprised of strolls around the campus. Sometimes, we would just go and sit on the shores of Lake Pontchartraine. One date in particular, I tied my wheelchair to her bicycle with a rope.

As we were making laps around the campus, onlookers would laugh and wave! On one of those laps, Renee dodged a killer pothole with her bike. The maneuverability of my wheelchair, however, led me to the center of the pothole which swallowed half my chair and sent me sailing on a trip for which I had not a ticket! Nothing was hurt but my pride! Renee's laughter made it worth it all!

One quiet evening, we were sitting on the back steps of my apartment building enjoying a rare, cool, clear evening of star gazing. I had brought a knitted afghan out to keep Renee warm. She was all snuggled up with my arm around her. When time came for her to return to her dorm room, she began to remove the afghan only to find that it had become entangled in her dental braces! There I was carefully detangling this concoction while trying not to damage her braces. Naturally, we both got the silly giggles but eventually, she was freed from the trap!

After a couple of months or so of these simple, special days of courting, I was dropping her off at her dorm following a pleasant evening meal together. I opened the door of my old Chevy pickup to let her out and there she stood in the moonlight smiling that smile at me! With all the courage I could muster, I told her I was old fashioned (which was my way of hiding my terror of being rejected) and I asked her if I could have the honor of kissing her goodnight? She said, "Please do!" I was so shocked that this vibrant, young, beautiful, fun woman actually wanted a kiss from the likes of me! As a matter of fact, I was so shocked that in a millisecond, I gave her a quick smack, jumped in my truck and drove off with her still standing there puckered up!!

It is a wonder she ever spoke to me again! Yet, it was her way of responding to that ever-so-abbreviated first kiss that points to the way her strengths embraced my weaknesses and channeled them to greater heights. You see, a few days thereafter, she stood facing me with that smile again! She put her arms around my neck and said, "Bryan, I want you to know that you can kiss me anytime you want!" Dear Reader, that second kiss was not nearly so abbreviated!! All of this may seem cute but trivial to some. However, Renee's embracement of me, weaknesses and all, was and continues to be a rocket-fired thrust of inspiration that keeps me going. I really believe that even if the whole world gave up on me, I could still fight onward as long as Renee believes in me.

Renee's greatest strengths are her love, steadfastness, persistence, patience and her contentment with what God provides. The depth of her spiritual foundation in the Lord exudes a strength that is immeasurable and uncanny. You see, I am known to be high strung. Most of the time, I am wound up tighter than a tick---sort of like a balloon inflated to the bursting point. It is a weakness of mine that relentlessly drives me to push onward in spite of my physical frailties. After operating like this all day, I will come home and I am still all wound up. But soon, I will hear Renee quietly humming a hymn and immediately, my RPM's begin to slow to a more humane pace. I will see her gently tending to our old, beat up tom-cat with a caring heart that is so rare nowadays. Such actions remind me to channel my energies upward instead of inward toward my weaknesses with which I struggle. Then later in the evening while I am toiling yet again in my study or over some other toilsome snare, she will quietly come up behind me, place her hands on my neck, shoulders and scalp and soon, this warring warrior is purring like that old tom-cat! Honestly, her effect on me during such times has led to my most effective sermon preparations.

Renee's quiet, inner strengths calm and soothe the warring and raging weaknesses with which I often grapple. I am convinced that God entrusts such strengths to only a precious, select few. I am so glad that He entrusted such to Renee because in so doing, God in His sovereignty guides and directs my weaknesses into and through His mighty hands enabling me to minister and pastor His sheep. This same guidance and direction overruled the medical claims that I would probably never marry and father children. Renee epitomizes all that motherhood should be and our two sons give proof of this blessed fact. Finally, in a way I cannot explain, Renee has become a mother of sorts to me since my own MaMa went to heaven. At times, I find myself referring to her as "MaMa" when I am talking to our sons. I remember my Dad referring to my MaMa in a like manner. I thought it odd and strange at first but now, I understand.

Renee's strength of drawing the best out of me is a priceless treasure. My fondest recollection of this strength came at my feeble attempt of proposing to her. I had waited until what I considered to be the perfect time and place. We had travelled to my home in Georgia during a break from seminary. I had grown up spending my fondest recreational times in the mountains. The Toccoa River is a very special highlight of the area for me. I have enjoyed many camping and tubing experiences in and along this river. One quiet and peaceful spot in particular on the bank of a tributary that empties into the Toccoa is where I took Renee that day. We sat there for a while on a blanket just soaking in the tranquility. Admittedly, I was a ball of nerves! I was so terrified that she would say no! Finally, I took her hand and I asked, "Well, will ya?" She answered, "Will I what?" I said, "You know?" She said, "What?!?!" I said, "YOU KNOW…WILL YA?!?!" She said, "You mean marry you?" I said, "YEAH!" She smiled and said, YES!!" To this day, she tells everybody that she had to propose to me!! That is fine! I will take her any way I can!!

The Wooing Power of Our Weaknesses

As I have tried to explain in previous chapters, God uses our weaknesses to stir to action the strengths within others. During the course of this writing, I witnessed anew the reality of this fact on an exceptionally huge scale. On 4/27/11, the Southeastern United States experienced a "super-outbreak" of tornadoes. These were not the typical, spring tornadoes from which we have learned to take cover over the years. Mississippi, Alabama and Georgia were placed under a PDS (Particularly Dangerous Situation) high-risk forecast by the National Weather Service. Unfortunately, their predictions were deadly accurate. Almost 300 people died within the aforementioned states. The vast majority was in Alabama. Within a radius of about seven miles from my home, over 50 people died. Even though all areas effected in Alabama are important to me, Tuscaloosa is especially so. My home is about six miles from "ground zero". An EF-4 rated super cell twister remained on the ground for about thirty minutes as it passed from southwest through northeast Tuscaloosa County. The monster storm was 1&1/2 miles wide and packed wind speeds of nearly 200MPH. The entirety of its path included businesses, homes, multi-family housing units, churches and government housing. Its edge hit Tuscaloosa's regional hospital, blowing out windows, removing awnings and, of course, causing a major power outage. The University of Alabama also suffered moderate damage. Countless trees were destroyed. Throughout the city, cars were thrown like trinket toys. Many, very substantial structures of all categories were literally removed from existence. The ones that remained in the storm path were either condemned as total losses and/or received very serious damage. The most horrid aspect of the losses of course was the human toll. In addition to the dead, those who remained were displaced much as an unwanted animal that has been thrown out in a desert place. They numbered in the thousands. In the first 24 hours alone, the hospital received 1000 injured patients. The number of casualties soon overwhelmed the hospital's morgue. My oldest son who is a surgical nurse was finally able to contact me to let me know he was OK. In his call, he said bodies were everywhere in the streets. The scene made an impression on him and on all who live and work in this area.

Words are always inadequate to describe such events. Cataclysmic, carnage, chaos, decimation, destitution are among the best terms I can muster. But through it all, two resounding traits were both brought to simultaneously coincide as never before in our state---weaknesses and strengths. In a matter of minutes, I saw a large portion of a vibrant, active city and county full of springtime hope reduced to an inability to help itself in the least of ways. In addition to the injured, there were masses of people who literally had nothing---no toothbrushes, no toilet paper, no clothes, etc. A place for them to sit and bleed and cry was a wrecked, overturned car or a downed tree. For those who had more than just a foundation where their home once stood, all that remained was crushed and twisted rubble similar to a landfill or a junkyard. Vast areas had no electricity, water or gas. For so many survivors, it seemed the world had stopped just one inch short of ending. All they had was their lives and it was this single, solitary living example of epitomized weakness that very soon caused the rising up of strengths from within people of all sorts.

Even from my own inherent weaknesses, strengths were called to task. My home and family were spared completely. Scriptures tell us, "…For unto whomsoever much is given, of him shall be much required…"(Luke 12:48b, KJV). I knew I had to help these folks, but how? I could not do construction work or run a chainsaw or perform any of the other manual labor that was sorely needed on a grand scale. Then came the call for help---the area nearest my home had the suffering who needed to eat. They needed non-perishable, ready-to-eat meals. Soon, my wife and I found ourselves joined together with hundreds like us. Together, we made meals consisting of peanut-butter and jelly sandwiches, chips, cookies, water and a Bible all contained in donated, reusable, insulated food containers. I got into my electric mobility chair and with my lap loaded down with these meals, I accompanied a team into the very midst of the disaster. There, we found the forlorn and the weak. Their gratitude was humbling. Their concern for others was mesmerizing as evidenced by the repeated times many of them refused food because they had already partook and they pointed us to those who had not. Therein, I witnessed strength emanating from the very depths of weakness itself.

Multitudes of teams from many states came and as of this writing, continue to come to do whatever they can to help. A group came from south Louisiana. They said, "Ya'll came to us when hurricane Katrina took us down, so now, we want to help ya'll." This same spirit also rose forth from the midst of one of college football's most fierce rivalries. In my opinion, the football rivalry between the University of Alabama and Auburn University is a global phenomenon. In an unprecedented occurrence, groups from Auburn University and Auburn fans from all over merged in Tuscaloosa to do all they could to provide relief. The immensity of the weakness that permeates this tornado disaster has caused to emerge from the core of a fierce rivalry a spirit of strength that transcends differences of all kinds. This strength meeting this weakness head-to-head and heart-to-heart is the very soul of all I seek to convey in this book. God takes the most unlikely of individuals in the midst of their most unbearable circumstances and unites them with the indwelling wealth of strengths of all sorts of people. Weaknesses initiate the release of strengths that otherwise may have gone unrevealed.

Only God can bring to fruition such uncanny strengths in the midst of unspeakable weaknesses. Throughout my day-to-day living experiences, I repeatedly encounter individuals from all walks of life who reach out to assist me. For example, those who open doors for me and my wheelchair have ranged from little old ladies to big, burly motorcyclists to children to you-name-it! Personally, I believe this is evidence of God's image in each and every one of us. Some reflect His image more readily than others. Either way, His image provides a bit of inherent good in every person. This image exhibits itself through strengths such as kindness, compassion, generosity, and selflessness to name a few. As I grow older and admittedly more needful due to my weaknesses, I am learning to swallow pride by allowing others to assist me when offered. Allowing their strengths to meet my weaknesses provides moments when both the giver and the recipient are found within God's hands to show forth His purpose in creating us to begin with---to help one another.

Thunder and Lightning

My two sons are the stuff of which dreams are made. As previously mentioned, early in my life, the doctors told my parents that I should probably never consider marriage or fathering a child. As best as I can figure, their bleak outlook on these topics was based on their expectations of my not living very long. As I lived onward, they adjusted their opinions to something that suggested that if I were ever to marry, I should probably never consider becoming a parent. Again, I do not know the basis of their opinion. Perhaps they were concerned of my producing another deformed child. Perhaps they were doubtful of my eventual parenting skills. As time and medical knowledge marched onward, concerns of my producing deformed offspring diminished to no more than the chances of this occurring from a deformed-free parent. The issue was a moot point as far as my wife and I was concerned. Understandably, both her parents and my parents obviously had reservations and so I consulted physicians regarding the matter. These doctors unanimously laid the matter to rest. Either way, Renee and I placed the matter into the Lord's hands. The results speak for themselves.

On December 11, 1986 and July 18, 1994, our lives and the world changed forever! These are the birth dates of our two sons, Ben and Zach. From the start, parenting was a natural calling for Renee. Her love and care for children was obvious way before we ever met. The rigors of pregnancy and all the challenges that have followed have brought the best out of her. All the strengths and treasures of a mother's heart have overflowed from her the past 25 years.

When it comes to parenthood, I was as green as they come! The extent of my babysitting experiences was keeping law and order among younger cousins, nieces and nephews. I had never changed a dirty diaper. Fortunately, what I lacked in skills I more than made up for with a strong stomach. As was the case for most things in my life, I learned to do as I traversed the various waters of child rearing. I never prayed for a boy versus a girl or vice versa. However, in His omniscience, God blessed me with boys because I honestly would have considered a girl too fragile for my unorthodox way of doing things.

Besides the obvious difference in their ages, our sons proved to be unique in the strategies of discipline required to guide them. I compare their differences with that between a semi-truck and a Corvette. Raising Ben was like driving a semi. He was always a chunk and grew into a formidable lineman for his high school football team. At 6'2" and 265 pounds, my Daddy exclaimed, "They didn't pick him green!" I grew up with the discipline of the belt. Yes, I got whooped (not whipped) when needed and you know what? I never needed rehabilitating because of it! This same method was utilized in raising my boys. Ben responded as expected in that through this physical stimulus, corrective actions were embraced. Just as it takes more effort to steer, maneuver and stop a semi as opposed to a Corvette, so too Ben (like his Daddy) required his extra share of "whoopings". Zach, on the other hand, responded in a very different way to being whooped. Even though he felt the physical stimulus, the effects soon proved to be detrimental in that these events would bruise his spirit to almost the breaking point. Just as a Corvette does not require air brakes to stop or thirty inch wheels to roll or a diesel engine producing a thousand pounds of foot-torque to move eighty tons, so too Zach proved to be much more responsive through the use of restrictions and/or loss of privileges. This revelation is tied directly to his "Attention Deficit Hyperactivity Disorder" or ADHD.

Once he was diagnosed, I learned to "drive" him like a Corvette as opposed to a semi. His "steering radius" was much tighter and more responsive to deprivations of his favorite activities. Thus, if his grades begin to fall, for example, he would be deprived of TV time or sports or time with friends. Such deprivations proved much more effective than being whooped.

Now, what does any of this have to do with weaknesses and strengths and this book in general? Plenty! Just as a semi and a Corvette have their own unique strengths and attributes, so too Ben and Zach have proven to be similarly so throughout our lives of interacting with one another. I will begin with Ben first.

Renee and I were serving at my first pastorate when Ben arrived. I was as prepared for this event as I could be. Physically, I was at my peak in life for most of Ben's childhood which was a special blessing because he and I were together as much as possible. At the end of most each day, I would take off my wooden leg and the living room floor would become a wrestling arena or a rodeo corral! Ben would ride his pet bull all over the house! He was always the champion wrestler. When he became a teenager, I purposely allowed him to come at me with all he had in order to allow him to vent the array of frustrations that accompany that age. Like I said, I am glad I was in good shape! After I was bruised enough, I would wrap him up and hold on until he was convinced we were done for the night! By the time I reached this phase of life with Zach, my physical frame required a different technique which I will explain later.

Aside from the obvious weaknesses rooted in my lack of parenting skills, my paranoia pertaining to Ben's safety was peaked from day one. This was first evidenced his fifth day on the planet. Following our return home after his birth, we noticed Ben was turning cantaloupe yellow. The doctors admitted us back into the hospital to treat Ben's imbalanced bilirubin levels. Twenty-four hours under the special lights and he was fine. But during those twenty-four hours, my paranoia reared its head to expose the weakness I never knew I had. While Ben was sleeping snug and warm under the lights in the infant holder there in our hospital room, feeding time rolled around. Renee calmly opened the holder's door and pulled the tray on which Ben was lying. To our horror, Ben rolled off the back side of the tray! I had been relaxing in a recliner without wearing my wooden leg. I stood up on my one leg in utter terror thinking Ben had gone all the way to the floor! Though startled, Renee knew he had merely rolled off of the tray onto another padded blanket tray. Ben barely let out a whimper and was soon contentedly enjoying MaMa's meal just for him! Most would say my reaction was understandable. However, this paranoia soon reared its head repeatedly after we returned home. If I heard Ben grunt, sneeze, burp or whimper, I went ballistic thinking a trauma was pending! However, it was Ben's natural infant's "strengths" that soon taught me a whole new dimension of trust in the Lord. Just as I knew I could calmly trust the Lord to tend to me in all my weaknesses, so Baby Ben taught me that he trusted in Renee and me accordingly and that I did not have to experience an hourly nervous breakdown to honor his trust. His trust was natural and in his fragile little frame, he harnessed my paranoia into a renewed trust of God Himself. As Ben and Zach both have grown, this renewal continues.

Being built as I am, I have grown accustomed to the curious stares of the public. However, when the Lord called me into the ministry, I soon realized I would often be on public display. Ben helped me to develop the proper approach to this matter in his early years. During his first few years of elementary school, Ben would often accompany me on visitation duties at hospitals and nursing homes. He usually led the way and would go right up to patients with a smile and his pleasant greetings. He did not try to be anything other than himself and in so doing, he taught me to do likewise throughout all endeavors of my ministry. Prior to this lesson, I would try to shroud physical frailties to the greatest extent possible and this only added to the dilemma of my weaknesses. As a child, Ben's approach challenged me to utilize my physical differences for the good of others and this approach has proven immensely beneficial and advantageous in ministry to others over the last 33 years. Now, I actually initiate and encourage others to inquire about my physical differences. I can no more hide them than one can hide thunder in a storm. From this conjecture, I affectionately refer to Ben as "Thunder". From early on, his open, vibrant personality would bring him onto any scene much as a clap of thunder! Now that he is grown, his tall, large frame and commanding smile still has the same effect.

In order to drive home Ben's thunderous liberation of my former weakness of trying to hide the inevitable, I share with you an event surrounding Ben when he was in preschool. We had just arrived inside his preschool facility on a stormy, spring morning. Suddenly, the tornado sirens blared and we found ourselves huddled in the hallway with teachers and students. Fortunately, we soon received the "all clear". In those days, my vehicle was a Chevrolet Suburban. As I bid goodbye to Ben and his friends and headed outside to begin my day of pastoral duties, Ben, who was very fond of our Suburban, shouted out loud in front of all the world who all knew I am a preacher the following question, "Daddy, ya gonna get the burban...ya gonna get the burban??" I responded, " Son, it's a Suburban, a Suburban!" Teachers were howling with hilarity at this preacher's embarrassment! Oh, life in the fishbowl is good! I have been the stronger for it ever since!!

My weaknesses have been approached by my younger son Zach much the same way lightning approaches its intended object: with blinding fervor that changes everything! Hence, his nickname of "Lightning"! Renee and I knew we wanted Ben to be a big brother. The gender of our second child was never a major consideration. As one year, then two years followed Ben's birth, we begin to wonder if child number two was ever to be. I am convinced that stress affects a couple's efforts to conceive a child. When Ben was fifteen months old, we left our first pastorate and moved to Tuscaloosa, Alabama in order for Renee to pursue a graduate degree from the University of Alabama. This move was as faith-based as you can get. Neither of us was employed. As I dispersed my resume' to prospective churches, I washed and waxed cars to earn money. Renee assisted her grandparents with harvesting a large garden. After a short stint of living with her parents, we bought and set up a 24 foot travel trailer for us to live in on her grandparent's property. This small space shrunk exponentially with our active toddler! It also did not lend itself to the privacy necessary for romantic interludes. Thus, time clicked on by with no second child. Eventually, I was called to my second pastorate and was working at the local rural water company while Renee went to school. In the meanwhile, we were able to purchase a used mobile home that was like a mansion compared to the travel trailer. Once Renee graduated, and was secure in her teaching career, we sold the old single-wide and bought a brand new double-wide in 1991. Things were looking up as was our hopes of having our second child. Two more years rocked by. Even though life's plate was more palatable, it was stacked high with stress. Finally, in the late fall of 1993, Renee, Ben and I took off for a few days of much needed recreation at my parents' cabin in the North Georgia mountains. Nine months later, lightning struck and Zach was born! We had no idea what a "bolt" he would provide in our lives.

Basically, he was sick the first eighteen months of his life with infected ears and all that goes with it. His nearly constant flow of congestion kept his stomach in a rage that made him vomit frequently. One particularly rough week when he was so sick, I had him lying on my chest in the recliner. Suddenly, I heard him make that unmistakable "urping" sound. To prevent him from choking, I held him up above my chest. Projectile puke jettisoned everywhere including into my shirt and yes, into my mouth! This was indeed a stellar test for my strong stomach. Seven year old Ben witnessed this whole fiasco! As the aroma of "upchuck" spread, Ben began to heave! I sternly told him to go to the bathroom and fill up the tub! This move both averted additional vomit and facilitated a major overhaul for Zach and me. This event and others like it added a new chapter to my counseling of prospective marital couples. I tell them, "A prerequisite to parenthood is developing the ability to hold a puking child steady on the toilet with one hand while using your other hand to eat a bologna sandwich!" After all, parents must maintain their strength!

Thankfully, Zach outgrew those early childhood miseries. His fragile frame in those first few years aroused a discipline over my own weaknesses as never before. I learned anew the Scripture's instructions of keeping our flesh in check (see I Corinthians 9:27, I Peter 2:11, Romans 8:1-8, 13:14 and 14:21). I knew I had it to do in order to be the husband and father my family needed. Little did I know that Zach's first few years were only a prelude to my weakness's greatest challenge as a parent. As Zach attended preschool, his energy levels began to soar to new heights. Throughout kindergarten and first grade, this energy was often a source of much frustration for his teachers, his peers and his parents. Renee's education and experience soon led us to have Zach tested. "Attention Deficit Hyperactivity Disorder" (ADHD) was the conclusion. Renee took a guarded but level-headed approach toward the recommended medicinal regimens prescribed for Zach. I took an approach of trying to be as supportive as my ignorance and inexperience would allow. At the same time, I had a hidden, inward approach that protested vehemently. I blamed myself and Satan almost had me convinced that something about my physiological differences brought this upon my son. My precious Renee even blamed herself as the cause due to the stress we allowed to intrude upon our lives throughout her pregnancy. She was terribly afflicted with morning sickness while pregnant with Zach. She even had a brief stay in the hospital to be rehydrated intravenously. Satan tried to tear us down as parents. In our weakened, exhausted state, he almost succeeded. Then, as Zach progressed in grade school, his energy levels were soon harnessed with the challenges imposed by increased academics. With many hours of perseverance and study, Zach has climbed the ladder and now enjoys his classes in high school. Also, from third grade through seventh, Zach excelled in the disciplines of Taekwondo Karate. He acquired the rank of second degree black belt. He "retired" from karate in the eighth grade in order to pursue his passion for football. As of this writing, he is in the eleventh grade and a fullback for his high school football team.

Just as a Corvette is fast and agile, so is Zach. Just as a Corvette can take you by surprise, so can Zach! Just as lightning has been proven to strike the same place more than once, so does Zach! As my body grows less mobile, I am stirred to greater heights by Zach's lightning-filled zeal for life. When he sees me struggling, he says or does something that is exactly what I need at the time. Sometimes, he may say something that makes me "mad as a wet hornet" but it will be just what I need to fight onward. At other times, he may come up behind me with a bear hug and no words at all and honestly, I feel I could plow up a 100 acre field with a spoon! I have witnessed Zach reaching out and helping others at times he did not know I was around. I have received reports from trusted adults who have admired him in similar respects. As preacher kids, both of my sons were shoved into the proverbial fishbowl of life. There, one has to choose between being a socialite or a hermit. I am so grateful that both of them chose to reach out and touch so many lives around them. As a nurse, Ben's effectiveness speaks for itself. As a teenager, Zach has rebelled against the stereo-typical "clicks" that often dominates his age group. Instead, he has friends of all shapes, sizes, races and economic backgrounds. Many of his peers do not understand Zach's forwardness toward others. I think his own words to me says it best, "Daddy, I'll hug a hobo!" I know Jesus is pleased with that. Personally, I am pleased, humbled and challenged to reach out and love folks like Zach does---without preconceived notions of fitting certain molds. This reality strikes me like lightning almost daily as the Lord places me into contact with so many needful people who do not fit the "church mold" that I am convinced sways so many lost people to stay lost.

I cannot leave my discussion of Zach without sharing about his God-given art talent. His artistic persuasion surfaced very early in life. Even his earliest art work expressed deep thoughts, concerns and impressive aspirations. In his art, he often reflects his concern for his family and me in particular. I am usually pictured in my wheelchair and my unique hands are highlighted. I am convinced this was his way of looking out for opportunities to help me and root me onward with my struggles and weaknesses. As he has matured, his art has done likewise. His attention to intricate details is awe-inspiring. The messages his latest works convey are ones that reflect a depth that few ever develop much less possess as a teenager. The ravages of the April 27, 2011 tornado in Tuscaloosa about which I shared earlier are depicted in one of his paintings used for the front cover of this book. In it, he has pictured the destruction and chaos and the horror it caused. However, throughout the picture, he has interjected messages of real hope that only God can give. As the twister fades away in the background sky, a rainbow masks the sky overlooking the scene. A sign lies on the ground with the inscription "John 14:6" imprinted on it as a message to all that no matter what happens, Jesus really is the way, the truth and the life. At the center of the picture is a broken, utility pole whose two pieces are entangled in the power lines, forming a cross. Zach and I were in the midst of this wreckage carrying food to the victims. I was overwhelmed by the loss and devastation. Zach also grieved over the scene but with a glorious twist that envisioned our healing, faithful, loving Heavenly Father in the midst of it all. Zach's painting tells of this. Such an uncanny, inner strength to derive at such a conclusion in the midst of such circumstances gives rise to Zach's source of real strength. In so doing, he naturally points others to the Lord without ever having to preach a word. As a preacher, I am often found agonizing over the right mix of words to sermonize. As a father, I find in my son Zach the strength to toil not over the wording but rather, allow the Lord to show Himself to be totally sufficient in all things. Indeed, there are those times during which there is strength in silence and solace in action. I will always be indebted to Zach for this lesson taught to me.

Finally, I hope and pray that I can someday be half the man my two sons have become and are becoming. Yes, they have called my faith to task as all children will. Both have totaled their first vehicles. Both have had their share of romantic heart-breaks. Both have received my wrath during the few times they were disrespectful towards their MaMa. However, both have afforded me rare moments of forgetting this weakened, fragile frame in which I am temporarily housed. During those times, I have hunted and harvested whitetail deer with my sons. I have watched them both excel in karate and football. I have witnessed both of them professing Jesus Christ as their personal Lord and Savior. I was blessed to baptize both of them. I often observe their unashamed stand for the Lord. At present, I am beginning to enjoy the pleasure of hearty, man-to-man conversations with them about all of life. Even though I may grow a little physically weaker with each passing year, I am made stronger in knowing that once I am gone, Renee is in the very capable hands of Jesus, Thunder and Lightning! Good God, I am so blessed!!!

Bryan and Renee Allen

Bryan's Parents, Billy and Betty Allen

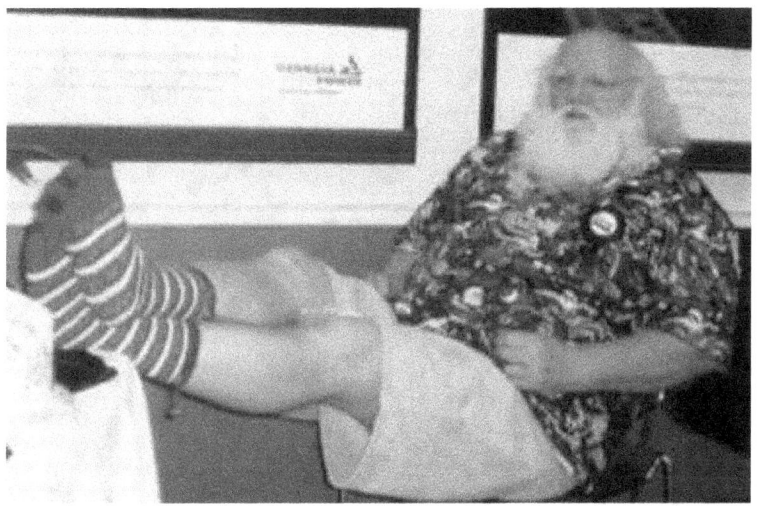

Bryan's Brother, Bill Odom

Bryan and his sons, Ben and Zach

Bryan's son, Ben

Bryan's son, Zach

Bryan and his sister, Diann Dilbeck

Tuscaloosa Tornado Damage
Zach Allen, Artist

Extra Mile Parenting

I suppose that next to my wife, my weaknesses highlighted my parents' strengths more than that of anyone else. In order to understand the extent of how their strengths were called to task by having a child like me, I struggled about whether I should devote a separate chapter to each of them or combine them into one. Since it took both of them giving it all they had to deal with all the special challenges I posed, I decided it best to keep them in one chapter. After all, it took both of them to make me! It took both of them to raise me. Now that they are together in heaven, I am convinced that together, they implore the Lord on my behalf from time to time. I know that may sound silly to some and unorthodox to others. However, their devotion and commitment to me and all the complications my physical differences presented would seem uncanny to some. Before they ever had any children, my parents decided that MaMa would stay at home and Dad would work outside the home. Granted, this may have caused a forfeiture of a few material things. For example, we never had a boat or an RV. We always bought used cars and kept them "forever"! I was 41 and well on my own before Dad ever bought their first brand new car. The largest house they ever owned originally had less than 1500 square feet and they paid a little more than $15,000 for it. That sum will not even buy an average priced car today! However, what we did not have materially speaking was more than countered by the gems we did enjoy: a clean house; home-cooked meals; eating together as a family at home; cherished, quality time often spent at home together. I remember watching MaMa cooking from "scratch". If she was mixing up something to make one of her glorious desserts, I licked the mixing bowl! If she needed meat ground up, I would crank the muscle-powered meat grinder for her. I would arrange and re-arrange her pots and pans. I would vacuum for her. When Dad returned home from work, I often would help him wash and wax our car. He pitched baseballs to me for hours. I always had a pedal car to ride in as a young child. Dad would get an old broom stick with a notch cut into one end. He would use it to push me all over the neighborhood. I remember at age four, I got away from him on a hill! I have never seen Dad run so fast! I thought it was great to drive that fast! All of these home-made activities and countless others caused me to never miss what so many others seemed to have. After I grew old enough to reflect back on things, I realize the extra expenses caused by my physical weaknesses prevented us from having some of the material extras. But what we did have could not be bought with money. I speak of a bond and cohesiveness that I honestly do not think would have been present without my physical differences and weaknesses. It was the concerted, unified, lifelong, God-centered efforts of my parents that made it all happen. Therefore, I will elaborate upon them individually while interjecting the role of both throughout my life.

I want to be clear that neither parent played a more important role than the other. Each possessed unique characteristics, strengths and even weaknesses of their own that proved to be the perfect fit for a child like me. Together, they were God's hands on this earth for me. They did for me what only two, God-fearing parents could do. They were sold out on making sure their children had the best done for them as possible.

Both of my parents were from the country. They were raised on farms amongst families with numerous children: ten on Dad's side and nine on MaMa's. There were more but some of their siblings did not live beyond childbirth and/or a few days. The frugality and thriftiness required for these two families to survive played a major role in my parents' rearing of their own children. Neither of them were stingy but both were resourceful and aggressively practiced the wisdom of "waste not, want not". They met in high school and wed on August 5, 1950. Dad was always straight and tall, dark hair, brown eyes and could have had most any gal he chose. Thankfully, he chose MaMa, a blue-eyed, light red-haired beauty that was definitely the pick among the six Dillard girls!

Dad was a career Navy man. He was shipped out two months after he and MaMa married. MaMa spent those early days with her parents on the old home place helping run the farm. She also was employed at W.T. Woolworth which, to my knowledge, was her one and only employ outside of the home. MaMa had her share of health issues but her resolve to take care of her family was instrumental in her mastering those issues. Then, I was born. My sister was born seven years before and my folks prayed for number two to be a son. Well, they got a son and a lot of extra baggage to boot! I will not repeat the particulars of my physical deformities explained earlier. Suffice it to say, the medical world in the fifties did not know a great deal about what to do for me or for my parents for that matter. The doctors held little hope that I would live beyond a year or so. Once two years passed, the doctors gave little hope for my mobility and thus, foretold of a grim future of being cared for as an invalid for the course of my life. When born, my hips were dislocated and a half body cast was applied in order to protect me from injury. In the meantime, the doctors were perplexed as how to correct my hips. They hoped that perhaps the cast would cause my hips to position correctly. However, x-rays were taken every few weeks and they showed no progress. As the doctors planned for what essentially would be an experimental surgery to correct the problem, they took one last series of x-rays. Soon after we returned home, the doctor called. MaMa answered the telephone. She and Dad were expecting to be told when to admit me to the hospital for surgery. Instead, the doctor told MaMa, "Mrs. Allen, we don't understand but Bryan's hips are back in their proper position." MaMa replied, "That's alright, doctor, we understand just fine!" You see, MaMa and Dad early on learned to rely on Dr. Jesus above all! Soon thereafter, the cast was removed and my hips have been back in their sockets ever since! This event was the first in a series of medical hurdles that we would encounter throughout my childhood and into my early teen years. Most of these hurdles involved experimental measures due to the unique nature of my situation. Both parents grappled with the conflict of protecting me from the uncertainties while letting go and letting God do His work.

The emotional struggles my parents endured due to my physical challenges were far-reaching. They hid their emotions from me for as long as possible in order to keep my childhood as joy-filled as possible. However, as I neared my teen years, I became quite sensitive to the strains they both bore on my behalf. I vividly remember the summer when I was six years of age. This was the summer my left foot was amputated. In those days, ether was the preferred anesthesia…preferred by the doctors at least! That stuff should be reserved strictly for cranking stalled tractors! I can remember that sickening smell. I vomited everything I had eaten my first six years of life! Soon after my release from the hospital, my stitches broke and this complication made a long, hot summer even longer. However, despite all the extra expense and trauma, the heat and pain of that summer was made bearable by my parents' purchase of our home's first air conditioner. It was a big window unit and it represented the essence of the sacrifice made by my parents for me throughout life.

I recall one day in particular that summer. My parents were afforded a much needed date-break while one of my aunts stayed with me. She and I conversed about the various events of that summer and how my surgery encompassed all activities at the Allen household. I remember my aunt telling me, "Bryan, your MaMa and Daddy love you so much…if they could, they would give you their feet!" Her words were so true. In the several years following that summer, I witnessed a gradual revelation of the ongoing heartbreak my MaMa experienced as she would watch me struggle along. Every childhood day was filled with tackling hurdles and obstacles. Doing so became second nature to me. However, negotiating the vast array of challenges my weaknesses presented was never accepted as second nature by my MaMa. As the years clicked by, I came to realize that MaMa was vexed with self-blame for my plight. Even though she took no medications during her pregnancy with me, still, she blamed herself. It was not until my last month at home before moving away that I realized the impact of her agony in all of this. For 23 years, she had at least been able to temper her self-blame by doing for me all she possibly could do to make life less of a struggle. But in December of 1982, she was grieving. She could not eat or sleep because that very month, I would be living 500 miles away in New Orleans. No longer could she wash my laundry and prepare my meals and tend to me as she always had. Her son, with all his needs, was moving out. It was then that she had to learn to do for me all over again what she had to learn to do for me at my birth---give me to the Lord. This proved to be an arduous process. My third month in New Orleans, I came down with the worst case of flu I have ever experienced. I did not dare let anyone back home in Georgia know of it. However, via a dream, MaMa knew I was sick. After being assured that Renee (my fiancé' at that time) and the campus physician were tending to me, MaMa conceded once again to give me over to the Lord. Granted, she has done so numerous times since.

Over the course of the next two years, I met, courted and married Renee. In December of 1986, Ben was born. During these four years, MaMa had very serious bouts with depression. She was diagnosed as manic-depressive/suicidal. She received shock treatments twice and was under the care of a psychiatrist the rest of her life. Through it all, a deeply suppressed struggle within her pertaining to me emerged.

She just never accepted the fact that I left home. Then when Ben was born, she saw in him all that she had hoped for in me and it was at that point that she really unraveled. The old saying, "some people have to hit rock bottom before they will look up", definitely applied to MaMa. It was not until she reached rock bottom, 27 years after my birth, that she ceased her focus of my weaknesses and instead, focused on all the Lord had prepared and allowed me to accomplish---primarily due to her and Dad's exemplary, sacrificial parenting. As she and Dad aged, health and mobility challenges of their own mounted, especially for MaMa. Her osteoporosis, double-curvature spine, disintegrating vertebra, and arthritic hips took their toll. Amazingly, during the few times that Dad got really down-and-out sick, MaMa's inner strength would emerge and arise to the task of caring for him in an uncanny fashion, similar to her care for me. During those times, she was able to suppress the great pain her body inflicted upon her and she would get the job done! When Dad would recover, she would begin to concede again to her frail frame. I am convinced that even up to the moment of her last breath, her inner strength that was fueled in her passion of caring for her own is the very element that kept her hanging on. When Dad, my sister and I whispered repeatedly in her ear that we were ok and she could go on to glory without worry, she did so very soon thereafter.

Despite MaMa's struggles, she maintained a dry wit and humor that kept all of us on the edge of our seats. We never really knew what she would come up with next! Her opinions were unvarnished to say the least! MaMa had the gift of accurately sizing up a person within the first few minutes of meeting them. She could spot a phony a mile away! On the other hand, if a person was sincere and genuine, MaMa would defend them like a female MaMa bear regardless of their popularity with the masses. She was a devoted Christian and faithful churchgoer. However, she knew true worth was not found in a parade of religious show and high-stepping theology. MaMa measured Godliness by the sincerity of one's care for others. Therein was found MaMa's greatest strength. It was so strong, in fact for me in particular, that it was almost her undoing as previously described. But as the years rolled by and Renee and I were blessed with yet another healthy son, MaMa embraced the gift and eventually shunned the self-blame, demonstrating a monumental strength. As I viewed her frail but pretty ninety pound remains prior to her burial, I thought---so weak, yet, how she had become so strong where it really matters. Her strength empowered me to cope with my physical weaknesses and challenges of aging and to fight onward so that she would not have to worry. I want to live in such a manner that when we meet again, she will be proud!

Dad was the tower of strength that every child needs. In his prime, I remember him carrying me on his shoulders. His 6'2", 240 pound frame of those days was imposing. I thought of him as my hero. As a career Navy man, he was always polished and sharp. He took me with him to the Navy base often. Everybody there respectfully referred to him as "Big A". I thought that was the grandest thing! We would get our military flat-top haircuts at the base barber shop. That was my hair style until seventh grade! Then and only then was I allowed to let it grow a bit...a very precious bit, I might add! As was the case with MaMa, I found in my later childhood years that Dad also had similar heartaches regarding my physical plight. Not for one second did he ever try to hide me from the crowd. He was so proud to have me by his side. With every medical hurdle, Dad was my coach, encourager, and at times, a military boot camp sergeant! Many uniformed sympathizers along the way took umbrage to Dad's persistent and sometimes aggressive approach toward me. Little did they know that his methods were exactly what I needed. They were unaware that his gentle hands rag-bathed me when casts and stitches prevented my getting into the tub. The several times during which I had to re-learn to walk, Dad's persistence, insistence, and motivation were just what the doctor ordered. However, I distinctly recall how this particular strength of Dad's had to be tempered a bit by my lead surgeon. Dr. King was a fine, Christian man and extremely talented in his field. He observed Dad's methods and my intense efforts to comply. Through his methods, Dad unknowingly exhibited a weakness in the midst of his strengths that the trained eye of Dr.

King could perceive. Dad wanted me to walk straight and tall. Dr. King knew that from a physiological standpoint, this was neither possible nor realistic. I remember standing before Dad and Dr. King. Dr. King would push his fingers into my lower side and he would guide Dad's fingers to the same point. He did so to show Dad that even though my hips were in socket, they were not in alignment and would never be unless a miracle occurred. This misalignment would always negate a straight and tall walk. I firmly believe that it was at that moment that Dad came to grips with the reality of my permanent imperfections. He was never in denial but he was always striving for me to succeed to the greatest extent possible. When he learned and accepted my physical limitations, he began to guide my rehabilitation efforts accordingly. Consequently, his strengths were made stronger by my incessant drive to overcome all that I could. My grappling weaknesses harnessed to his compassionate strengths to drive me onward made quite a team. It all helped Dad to deal with reality while helping me overcome.

Admittedly, Dad struggled with my physical weaknesses until his dying day. He knew I had peaked in my physical achievements prior to my thirtieth birthday. From that point, his pursuit was to keep me from losing ground. But as predicted by the doctors early on, my unusual physical stature, along with the normal wear and tear of aging, caused my lower extremities to deteriorate. My dependence on a wheelchair increased gradually with every passing year. Now, I am 90% dependent on a wheelchair. In fact, I have one manual chair, two electric mobility chairs and a van equipped with a chair lift. Ironically, it was Dad who encouraged my use of a mobility chair. He was most concerned over the filth that touched my hands when using the manual chair. His concerns were substantiated only a couple of years ago when for no apparent reason, my left hand, comprised solely of one finger, became infected. The doctor had to cut it open to allow the infection to drain. It soon healed. Soon, I began to make frequent use of my mobility chair. By the way, my first mobility chair was bought and given to me by my sister. Dad soon bought me another just so I would have a spare. My decision to buy the van was an arduous ordeal because I loved my pickup. However, if Dad could swallow his pride regarding my plight, I again was compelled by his example to do likewise. Dad died several months after I purchased the van. His provision for my sister and me allowed me to pay the van off three years in advance! He was always looking after me.

I conclude this chapter by sharing a very touching scene that occurred on my fourteenth birthday. I was scheduled for admission to the hospital for major, reconstructive surgery on my right (and only) foot. I briefly mentioned this event earlier. This surgery was highly experimental. A similar attempt was made to correct my foot when I was an infant. The procedure did not work. Fourteen years later, study had encouraged the doctors to believe they could accomplish a great deal with new surgical techniques. My bags were packed and in the car. Just as we were about to exit the house, Dad stopped MaMa and me for a moment of prayer. I sat down in one of the kitchen table chairs. Dad knelt on his knees in front of me holding my hand and MaMa's hand. He began to pray and then the words stopped as he wept. Finally, the words came: "Lord if the doctors mess up, please correct it." Yet again, I saw a level of strength exhibited by my Dad, a strength that could move mountains. The only way he knew how, he gave me and all of my frailties to the Almighty and simultaneously to the doctor's care as well. Only after I became a parent did I come to realize the strength required to pray such a prayer. The only way to allow your child to enter into a chapter of life with so much uncertainty and risk is by giving them over first to Him who is fully certain, who is without risks, and who changes not. Without that prayer of commitment, I would never been able to endure the next three months.

The pain of reconstructive surgery proved to be horrendous. It far excelled the pain of my amputation eight years prior. Before I could be released from the hospital, I had become too dependent upon pain killers. I literally had to go through withdrawal. I remember lying flat on the hospital bed. Without warning, I would convulse from head to toe so violently that I would literally jump horizontally off the mattress only to come crashing back down. Such episodes made my encased, bandaged, newly reconstructed foot throb horribly. Finally after three days of this, I was able to go home.

The next three months involved excruciating healing and rehabilitation. A custom shoe was made for my new foot. I long awaited the day to put it on so I could stand up and walk. Upon attempting my first step, I fell flat on my front side! Much to my dismay and surprise, the new foot at the end of my leg did not match with the old foot that was still in my brain. I literally had to train both mentally and physically to walk. My Dad built a straight walking lane with hand rails. He placed it in the driveway. From dawn to dusk, for four weeks, I sweated and struggled up and down those rails. Every time I would attempt to let go of the rails, down I would go. Finally, one Sunday morning after church, we returned home. Dad had helped me out of my wheelchair onto the living room sofa. Soon, MaMa called us to the dinner table. With virtually no premeditation whatsoever, I arose from the sofa and walked from there into the kitchen without holding to a thing! When I rounded the corner from the living room into the kitchen, my Dad was putting ice into glasses for the sweet ice tea. When he looked up and saw me, he shouted, threw ice everywhere, and grabbed MaMa! She began to holler! I forgot about eating! I was going for a walk! There I went all through the house, into and out of every room! I did not even want to sit down long enough to eat! That night at church, I walked into the sanctuary! The whole place celebrated!

Indeed, that was a high point for my family and me. We have often reflected on that event to draw strength for the potpourri of challenges that the years would bring. That day is exemplary for demonstrating how the weak things in the hands of God will flourish if they remain there long enough. The vast array of glaring weaknesses with which

h we wrestled my fourteenth year called to task every ounce of strength within my parents. I know their rewards in glory were increased manifold for all their sacrifices on my behalf. Their doing so has enabled me to reach people for the Lord in the Gospel ministry for the last 33 years. What an awesome day it will be when in glory, I will walk straight and tall with my MaMa and Daddy! I will even have a foot race with my two boys and since there are no losers in heaven, we will all three win!

The Call of Sister

Relationships between siblings are highly varied. This variation ranges from a total denial of existence between the siblings to an inseparable connection that transcends all differences and distances. I am very thankful the relationship between my sister and I definitely leans toward the latter extreme. Diann was born seven years before me. From the start, she was the caring big sister. I have often looked fondly upon the old black and white photos of us when I was just a baby. I guess one bright spot in my lack of mobility was the convenient excuse it gave Diann to tote me around! I was her living toy doll with whom she played and for whom she provided her constant care and protection. Now, fifty-three years later, much of that instinctive care-giving is still within her. When I go to visit her, I can scarcely lift a rag to blow my nose without her moving into position to assist! I have to remind her to calm down …I got it! The natural, mother's love and all that goes with it was bred into Diann. Both our parents came from homes with exemplary mothers whose care for their own was totally selfless and sacrificial. Diann had great teachers from early on and I was the fortunate recipient of all her sweet offerings!

All of the extra attention and resources my needs required of our family could have easily embittered Diann with jealousy and envy. If ever there was a shred of either, she kept it well hidden. As I grew into a toddler and through kindergarten, Diann would often dress me up like a big, girl doll named Jesserine! She has pictures of this that could easily be used as formidable blackmail material! I did not mind any of this at first but as I got older, I stopped it, much to her chagrin!

Our relationship prior to my becoming a teenager was typical of two siblings who were seven years apart and of different genders. I was all about cars and trucks. She was all about dolls, kittens and such.

We did enjoy an occasional board game. We often played church. I was the preacher who would throw hymnbooks at the congregation full of stuffed animals as I preached many hell-fire-and-brimstone sermons! Diann was the pianist! Despite all this fun, the natural conflicts arose and our relationship took a pivotal turn for the better one day when I was about ten or eleven. We had been picking on each other on a grand scale that day, so much so that it turned physical! Diann bopped me on the head with a pancake skillet! Once I had gained my bearings, I planned my revenge! In those days, if I was just chilling out at home, I would leave my wooden leg off and move around the house on "all fours". I hid under the dining room table waiting for Diann to come out of her room which was located at the farthest end of the house. The hallway began at her door. Finally, she came out. I charged at full gallop to my unsuspecting victim! I plowed between her legs with both my shoulders clipping both of her knees. I am not sure of the number of flips she turned before hitting the hardwood floor. However, the results were two-fold. First, she did not hit me with a skillet or anything else ever again! Second, Daddy whooped my butt profusely! No, I did not offer him an explanation for my actions. Diann felt so bad about the whole thing that from that incident forward, our relationship became much more civil. I suppose her dating years beginning along that time had something to do with it since we saw less of one another. Then the day came that she got her first car…a CAR! This car was a real, tangible object of connectivity between her and me. On Sunday afternoons, we would go cruising. Her ride was a 1966 Chevy Impala coupe with a "turbo-fire" V-8! I never told Dad about her blowing the doors off a '64 Chevy one Sunday! What fun! The eight-track would play Beach Boys music. The windows were down and the wind blew our hair! Our final stop would usually be Dairy Queen for a chocolate-dipped cone! Now that is living large!

Soon, I was a senior in high school. Diann was married and expecting her first child. I would vacuum and dust for her when she was well into her pregnancy. In turn, she would cook. She inherited that talent from MaMa too! Like us, Diann's daughter and son are several years apart with the daughter being the oldest. I love my niece and nephew dearly. I recall a most touching scene with my niece when she was just a toddler. I was still living at home with my parents. One evening, I was about to take off my wooden leg when she came bounding into my room. I quickly grabbed a bed sheet to cover myself but my wooden leg was still unveiled. She came over to me, stared at my wooden leg and asked, "What's dat?!" I replied, "Uncle Bryan's wooden leg." "Why is it like dat?" she asked as she patted its hard surface. I answered, "It helps me to walk." As she looked up at me intently, she leaned over, kissed my wooden leg and scampered off to play elsewhere! I was stunned, humbled and moved beyond words. I was so afraid she was going to be afraid of me or think I was a monster. Instead, she embraced me for who I am; weaknesses and all. From that day until this very day, we refer to each other as "Bestest Buddies!"

Now, how does all this tie in to my weaknesses and my sister? For one thing, I am convinced that our close relationship directly affected how things have panned out between Diann's children and me. Up to that event with my niece, I had done my best to avoid younger children because frankly, my physical differences were often more than most of them could handle. I recall numerous times when children would see my hands or my unusual walking gait and they would either run away in fear or point in a mesmerized stupor with their mouths hanging open! My niece and nephew grew up around me observing how close their mother and I were. Therefore, they knew I was harmless …crazy but harmless! All of this revolutionized my approach toward interacting with children once I entered the Gospel Ministry. From that point until today, I practically go out of my way to interact with a child, albeit with enough caution so as not to alarm them. I welcome their candor and raw honesty! I am intrigued by how some of them will walk right up to me and ask with wide eyes, "What happened to your hands?" Some even take my hands in their own hands for a close-up, personal inspection! Their responses have been varied. I recently had one inquisitive little girl declare about my hands, "That's ugly!" Others repeatedly ask, "Does it hurt?" Most ask things like, "Why are you that way?" or "How do I do this or that?" They really look in awe when they see me write or drive a car!

Diann's early intervention with me was a major catalyst for all of this. So many others with physical birth defects with whom I come into contact never rise above being withdrawn from others. Diann was really the first kid to play with me and because of doing so, I learned to play with others. Others would soon learn that I was interested in kid stuff too! I just went about doing things differently. From about age twelve to fourteen, the neighborhood kids wanted me to play football with them. Of course, they knew that running was not an option for me. However, by that age and even until now, I possessed exceptional upper body strength. Therefore, we would play football on our knees! The ball was always handed off to me. I would plow along on all fours with three or four defenders riding my back who were always unsuccessful in their attempts to tackle me down! They called me "TANK"! Those were fun days! They were spearheaded by my sister who early made it her mission for me to have fun and to do so with others. Her personality has always been outgoing, vibrant, bubbly and hilarious at times! Thankfully, it proved to be infectious for me. Now, in these mid-life days of managing new mobility hurdles, I see the hilarity in it all. Yes, I do laugh at myself! Sometimes, when asked what happened to my fingers, I reply, "This was caused by my picking my nose as a child...my fingers fell off!" Of course, I always follow up with the truth but if I were a gambler, I would bet that a host of young'uns have given up snot and buggers thanks to me!

As can easily be imagined, Diann and I are still kids at heart when we are together! Many people say that we communicate in our own alien language with each other! That is hard to explain. You just have to experience it! The best times come when she has cooked my favorite, gas-producing foods! Honestly, the older I get, the less it takes to launch my talents of flatus! Diann responds by unloading a can of Lysol!

Granted, our closeness has bonded even closer over the years as we faced some trying times. Diann's divorce from her children's father was the first, really big trial. The era in which we were raised considered divorce for any reason to be taboo. Because of that view and a variety of other reasons, I made it my mission to come to her defense against the tongue-waggers and their pious judgments of my sister. I was and remain prepared to place my wooden leg beside some craniums if necessary to defend Diann! Fortunately, it has not reached that extreme...to date!

After several lonely years, Diann met and married a fantastic guy named Billy. What a guy! He loved my sister! He loved my parents! They loved him! Also, he loved cars and he even raced at the local track on Saturday nights! Talk about connectivity! He and I were never short on material to discuss. I was blessed to officiate their wedding. Unfortunately, several years after they married, Billy was diagnosed with cancer. The battle was hard fought by him and Diann. During that time, Billy was reduced from being a strong, robust diesel mechanic to a man who could not even feed or bathe himself. Diann's care for him was second to none. The care she invested in me in my early days resurged during Billy's last months of life. Her strengths arose to meet his weaknesses in ways that only the Lord Himself could enable. In the midst of it, Billy's immeasurable love for Diann emanated from his sick and fragile frame. His love for her fueled her strength and love to care for him.

After Billy died, I found myself wanting to load Diann up and bring her to my home. The past 33 years in the ministry has taught me a thing or two about dealing with grief. However, I felt so helpless to help her. In so many ways, questions of "why" and "how" arose. I longed for sufficient answers but there were none. So, in all of my newfound inability to help, all I could do was to be there and listen to Diann with an open mind, a crusty ear, and a strong shoulder. I do not know if I did her any good but the special stuff she is made of has emerged and she copes with ups and downs. Through it all, we have become closer than ever.

Finally, our lives were simultaneously changed forever during a two-year period during which our parent's health declined and they both died within six months of each other. Lengthy illnesses and the subsequent process of settling estate affairs have been the demise of many sibling relationships. Thankfully, all of this made our bond stronger. There was never the first squabbling word between us. Even in the midst of so much personal loss, our personal weaknesses that caused us to fall so short in being able to fully grasp the loss of our parents was met by God's strength which in turn made stronger our sibling bond. I suppose this is yet another strange working of God in that He took the worst of times and used it to forge two people tighter than ever at the very point of their weaknesses and losses. By His so doing, Diann and I are the stronger for it all. Only the hands of God can turn it out this way!

The Call of Brother

Biology and bloodlines are by no means the only requirements to create a sibling. Even though I have only one biological sibling, my family and I were blessed and favored by God with a man who indeed stays closer than a brother. His name is Bill.

When I was ten, a young family purchased a home, two houses down from my childhood home. They had a very young daughter so I figured there would be no potential for the development of automotive interests. I was often found riding my three-wheel, adult bike that my parents sacrificed for me to have and enjoy. While riding one evening, I happened to be in front of Bill's house when he arrived at the end of the work day. He had a red, Plymouth Valiant that I admired. He got out of his car, saw me staring at his car and he said, "howdy". I spoke and complimented his car about which we conversed a few moments. Then, he went into his house.

Soon, I began to notice Bill would often come home in a different car. Naturally, this stirred my interest. I made it a point to be within sight of his house about the same time every evening to see what he would be driving. Bill was the sales manager of a large tire company in Atlanta. Customers would entrust him to pick up and deliver their cars which he would drive to his home. I had the awesome experience of having close-up views of all types of cars! In the midst of this experience, Bill noticed me washing and waxing my parent's cars. He asked me if I would be interested in earning some money by washing and waxing his cars. He even allowed me to drive them from his house to mine and then back to his once the work was completed. Even though this was a round trip with a grand total of 500 feet, it was extra cool for me as a boy! My Dad had taught me the art of hand-washing and waxing a car--- no electric buffers allowed! Soon, Bill spread the word and I had a nice side-job going! I charged $10-$15 per car, depending on its size. Inevitably, customers would tip me a few dollars. Most Saturdays were spent from dawn to dusk on my job. Usually, I could complete two cars. That usually meant I had $40-$50 in my pocket by day's end! That was big money for a twelve year old kid in those days!

Bill had a special love for VW's, especially the Beetles. He has owned at least a dozen of them over the years! One in particular was red with mag wheels. The red paint was faded and I told Bill I believed I could bring some shine back into that old bug if he would trust me to use some polishing compound. He agreed and the red bug soon sparkled! It opened up a whole, new phase of my business. People were glad to pay me an extra $20 to compound their faded paint and this was in addition to the wash and wax job! I was in the money!

All of this business sparked a lifelong relationship between Bill, my family and me. Admittedly, Bill was intrigued with the work that I accomplished despite my physical challenges. Others were apparently impressed as well. I was blessed to have customers who entrusted cars to me that I could only dream about---Cadillacs and Lincolns! In the midst of all this activity, Bill and my parents became acquainted. Bill was a deacon and a Sunday School teacher in a local church. These positions especially impressed my Dad! Unbeknownst to me, Bill had been asking my Dad about allowing me to come camping with him and his brother. My physical challenges never lent themselves to such activities before but Bill was insistent that it would be a good experience. He was right. In fact, camping has become a lifelong love for me. In addition, river tubing also became a passion that opened up new avenues for me to negotiate my weaknesses and physical challenges on a grand new scale. This recreation taught me some valuable lessons regarding my use of humor to deal with my weaknesses. I am forever indebted to Bill for facilitating this lesson.

For example, when tubing, we often encounter some of the mountain homesteaders that live along the Toccoa River in the North Georgia Mountains. These people are the salt of the earth and to this day, many of them survive quite well with only a minimal contact with the outside world. On one tubing trip in particular, we were deep within the mountain ranges when we floated within sight of an old, inhabited cabin. An elderly lady heard our "hootin" and "hollerin" and made her way down to the river to investigate. When I tube, I leave the wooden leg at camp which provides me with an empty britches leg. When we were close to the lady, I grabbed and violently shook my empty britches leg while shouting, "I lost my leg on those last rapids! Help me! Oh no! I lost my fingers too!!" The poor, old lady's mouth hung open in desperation! Bill shouted to her, "Ma'am, if you see a leg or some fingers float by, just gather them up and we'll pick them up on the next trip!" Bless her heart! She headed back to her cabin and we assumed she may have been on her way to get a shotgun! Thus, we sped up our paddling efforts!

One day, my dependence on a wheelchair proved to be a weakness that lent itself to a grand moment of hilarity! Bill and I had been horsing around in a large shopping mall. Finally, we settled down to do some leisurely window shopping. Suddenly, we found ourselves at the wide-open entrance of "Frederick's of Hollywood". This is a store that sells all manner of ladies lingerie and underwear most of which are comprised solely of dental floss and single-ply bathroom tissue! Bill had been behind me pushing the wheelchair. Without warning, he grabs the chair, turns me straight into Frederick's and gives me a resounding, heave-ho shove into a rack of very skimpy apparels! Being a single, virgin male, I had no idea that such attire existed! At that particular point, I did not care! All I had on my mind was revenge! I tore out of that store on one wheel hollering, "I'm gonna kill him! I'm gonna kill him!" Unbeknownst to me, during my rage, my wheelchair and I left that store with all manner of merchandise tangled and attached to me and the chair! A store clerk ran behind me shouting, "Sir, you have to pay for that stuff!" I soon saw Bill who had taken refuge in the midst of a group of children. He knew I would not harm them and therefore, stood there grinning at me in safety! In the meantime, the store clerk was gathering and detaching merchandise. When she asked if I intended to purchase any of it, I just glared at her! She quietly returned to her store with no further commentary. All this is funny …now! Time has a way of putting things into perspective!

Before I share on a more serious note, I must share one more humorous event. Bill and I were taking a jaunt through the mountains in one of his VW Beetles. We were admittedly negotiating the curvy route at a faster speed than the law allows. After screaming around one, long curve, we entered a rare straight stretch. Suddenly, the rear end of the old car jolted up and down. To our amazement, as we kept rolling, the left rear tire went past us as if we were parked! In the meantime, I was holding on for dear life in the midst of a fervent, prayer moment while Bill wrestled to regain control. When we finally slid to a sideways halt, we just sat there for a moment trying to collect our wits! I opened my door to get out. When I did, I noticed my foot had no ground on which to stand! I leaned over and to my horror, all I could see were clouds and a drop with no bottom in sight! We had stopped on the very edge of a cliff overhang! Unable to speak, I grabbed Bill, pulled him over my lap with his head hanging out the passenger door. When I pulled him back in, he was white as a ghost and barely breathing! He ever-so-gingerly moved the old bug away from the cliff. The tire had rolled to a stop and fell onto its side about fifty feet from the car. It too was on the edge of the abyss! While Bill retrieved the tire, I removed one lug nut from each of the other three wheels and tightened all the remaining lug nuts! After Bill mounted the tire, we drove home under the speed limit and with words of prayerful praise being the only words we spoke!

When I turned fifteen, Bill's life came apart at the seams. By then, he had two young daughters whom he adored and they were likewise towards him. Unfortunately, divorce ripped him apart from his children and from there, Bill began a long, downward spiral. Having lost his sales management position, he found himself working an inhumane number of hours at two minimum wage jobs in order to meet child support payments. Half the time, his old VW would not crank in the mornings and I would go and jump it off so he could go to work. Soon, Bill made a recluse of himself. He blamed himself for his dilemma. He was especially distraught over the thoughts of losing his girls and not being able to see them again. He feared they would grow up to hate him. Soon, Bill alienated himself from everyone, including me. We had become best friends and I commenced a search to find him. Eventually, I located him in a boarding house. His diet consisted only of water, peanut-butter and crackers. He was still working both jobs. He was reduced from a strong, witty, vibrant man to a mere shadow of his former self. He was sick and miserable. After I told my parents what I had found, they said to bring him home.

Afterward, Bill frequented our home. There, he found MaMa's wonderful cooking, Dad's wise counsel and me. Despite my physical challenges, for a time I was the stronger of the two. Bill would tearfully confide in me. With Bible in hand, I would pray for him and push him to man-up to be what I knew him to be. Granted, it was an up and down process for Bill. Despite the fact that his lonely heart was broken, it was still as big as ever and yearned to give as only a loving husband could. At first, he misdirected his yearnings toward female companions that could never provide the quality of heart, soul and companionship Bill longed for and deserved. His second marriage seemed hopeful at first but soon ended in more despair and bitterness. Bill was now convinced that no one could or would ever want him. At that time, I as a teenager had similar thoughts toward the opposite sex, albeit for different reasons. Every time I would dare to go beyond a casual friendship with a girl, they would soon become standoffish. I know my physical differences were the cause and so I just quit trying. However, in my eyes, Bill had no excuse to give up. As I prayed, God scolded me. He made it clear that if I would not trust Him for a companion, I had no business telling Bill to do likewise. Together, Bill and I learned to trust God anew in this matter as well as in a host of others. In time, Bill met, courted and married Amy. By then, Renee and I were happily married and raising our family. I was pastoring my second church. Bill and Amy visited with us one Sunday morning. Following that service, we had their wedding complete with a reception provided by some of the faithful ladies of our church! Bill and Amy are still happily married and enjoying retirement. Bill had been hired by a major electric utility where he remained employed for many years, providing finances for a comfortable retirement.

I must include the following, blessed segment about Bill. To date, he has been playing Santa Claus for over forty years. He has the real beard, hair and belly! He even has a real Mrs. Claus—Amy! What an awesome duo! Together, they minister not only to bring Christmas joy but to share the real meaning of Christmas at all of their engagements. They make sure to emphasize that Jesus really is the real reason for the season. They do this in homes, businesses, hospitals, retirement homes and even schools!

God has worked an amazing transformation with Bill throughout our friendship and brotherhood together. I proudly introduce him as my brother! Together, we grappled with each other's weaknesses and trials in the providence and power of the Almighty God through His Son and our Savior Jesus Christ. Even though age and mileage has made us both weaker and fatter, I am confident in saying that spiritually, we are two old buzzards who fly high on the wings of eagles! We still push one another up during the trials of life. Bill's zest for life and his selfless heart compelled him to give me a chance long ago when cleaning cars was my passion. As my passions changed to those of serving the Lord, Bill has repeatedly facilitated ways for me to expand my service to the Lord. He has done this primarily by connecting me with people and churches that needed to hear and know that God is indeed God of all, including God of the weak things!

The Call of Work

To set the proper tone for explaining the role that work has played in my life of overcoming weaknesses, I offer these verses of Scripture (all cited from the KJV):

> "...if any would not work, neither should he eat."
> (II Thessalonians 3:10b)

> "...study to be quiet, and to do your own business, and to work with your own hands."
> (I Thessalonians 4:11)

> "Be ye strong therefore, and let not your hands be weak: for your work shall be rewarded."
> (II Corinthians 15:7)

> "Whatsoever thy hand findeth to do, do it with thy might..."
> (Ecclesiastes 9:10a)

My life has proven to be a constant effort to accomplish as much as possible with what I have. Physically, this effort has required me often to put forth at least twice the effort to accomplish what the normal-bodied person would achieve. Understand that I am not complaining. This exponentiation in effort has become commonplace for me. I know no other way. Now past the typical half-way point in my life, my body increasingly offers protestations of the rigors I have and continue to put it through. So be it! It has been and continues to be quite a ride and when I go out, I will definitely do so with my boots on!

From my earliest days of childhood play to the present, mobility issues and/or all activities beyond the purely mental have encompassed a vast array of improvising. My methods have not always been orthodox nor are they always laced with finesse', grace and beauty. The prime example would be my egress and exit from a chair. This process involves (what to the beholder appears to be) a series of contorted yoga moves that focuses on how far out my butt can protrude without actually detaching from my thorax! Like I said, it is effective but not pretty! Thus goes the gist of most of my doings. Nevertheless, doing I have, doing I do, and doing I shall until there is no more to be done! I have never, nor will I ever, use my physical weaknesses and challenges as an excuse to not work and do and live life to the maximum! Understand, if a person unequivocally and undeniably has a providentially hindering impediment that prevents them from working, then my prayers are with them. However, from my unique perspective, a weakness or handicap or whatever you want to call it should never be embraced as an excuse to sit on the stool of "do nothing" while whittling on the stick of "do less". Instead, embrace the greater and much more fulfilling challenge of adopting weaknesses/handicaps in the midst of fulfilled living, rather than just existing.

I suppose this adaptation can be best illustrated by my earliest efforts of employ as a youngster. In addition to the car washing/waxing business explained earlier, I devised another moneymaker that was fun as well. I had an adult, three-wheel bicycle. With the use of some scrap lumber, and a discarded golf-club-bag-cart-chassis, I made a trailer that towed behind my bike. I used this rig to haul away leaves, tree limbs, and all manner of refuse. At the end of my neighborhood was a large, undeveloped area of wooded acreage. Therein were miles of bicycle trails and they led to several appropriate areas for discarding biodegradable items. To negotiate these trails in all kinds of weather, I mounted a pair of motocross tires on the rear of the bike (trike actually). It proved to be almost as agile as a Jeep! I could even haul other kid's bikes out of the woods when they broke down!

Now all this may sound like child's play. However, in light of the fact that the idea of my doing anything like riding a bike was written off as impossible at my birth, I would respond with a resounding "BALONEY" to the child's play surmise! Besides, it was work and I got paid for it! "Nuff" said! Even during those times when I had to convalesce following surgeries, I was mastering the hobby of building model cars. At one point, I had over one hundred model cars! In light of my hands, many observers remain skeptical that I was the builder. However, there were more than enough witnesses to vouch for me. Even though this hobby was no moneymaker, it preserved my work ethic during those periods of my life when mobility was most limited.

My love for cars and all things pertaining thereto drove me early to desire a livelihood as a master mechanic. I enjoyed accompanying my Dad's colleagues who patiently allowed me to get in their way under the hood of whatever they were repairing. As a teenager, Dad observed my struggling and straining while working on cars. I never considered it to be a problem. However, in his wisdom, Dad looked ahead thirty or forty years. One day, he sat me down for a heart-to-heart talk. He explained to me the inevitable likelihood of my physical mobility deteriorating on an increasing scale as the years would progress. Because of this likelihood, Dad looked me in the eyes, knowing my passion for cars, and said, "Son, you're going to have to earn your living with your mind and heart, not your body." As devastating as it was to hear that, deep down, I knew he was right. Now in my fifties, I know it more than ever. Thus from that point onward, cars were no longer my prime directive. I had to find a replacement.

After being awarded an academic scholarship to attend college, I commenced my undergraduate studies in Business Management and Finance. During my junior year in college, I began circulating my resume' in search for my first "real" job. Soon, I received numerous contacts of interest many of which led to interviews with prospective employers. It did not take many of these interviews for me to notice the reservations upon the faces of the interviewers. Soon, these reservations would lead to questions such as, "Can you write?" or "Can you use a typewriter or computer or telephone, etc.?" These questions may have been remotely justifiable had these people not had my resume' in their hand which detailed my abilities. After about the forth interview of enduring this nonsense, I made up my mind to handle things differently during the fifth interview. Sure enough, the same type questions commenced. I stopped the comptroller who was interviewing me and I told him, "Sir, I will take this office apart and put it back together again if you so desire!" For a moment, he looked at me in flabbergasted amazement as his mouth hung open! His next words to me were, "You're hired!" The reader needs to understand that this first job was for a very, well-known global company! Finally, my glaring weaknesses proved to be a major strength and advantage for me. Following my graduation from college, I left this first employ for another larger company and remained there until I left for seminary.

Upon reflection, I realize those early days of job searching proved to be a training ground and an education as well. I learned that no matter how impressive my resume' and its references made me appear to be, still I looked very weak and incapable in the eyes of the beholder. This initial impression is undeniably a weakness I know that I will have to overcome repeatedly until heaven is my home. I also know that my only hope of accomplishment is by the grace and strength of Jesus Christ. Dad was right. No one in their right mind would hire me for my body! Thankfully, each and every employer who hired me did so in part despite my body. They knew I had "it" on the inside and my body proved to be a driving force to unleash my inner attributes. Again, God proves Himself in strange ways at times. He continued to do so as I embarked upon my call from Him to preach the Gospel.

As is the case with most seminary graduates, I circulated my resume' far and wide as graduation approached in May of 1985. That day came and passed with no church to pastor. Renee and I moved in with her parents. She assisted her grandparents with their gardening and the subsequent harvesting/canning efforts. I washed and waxed cars and preached on a supply basis when called upon. Late that summer, I began receiving inquiries in response to my resume'. In September of 1985, Valley Head Baptist Church in Valley Head, Alabama called me as their pastor. No words of gratitude could ever be adequate enough for this opportunity. This congregation looked beyond two major points and called me anyway. First, I had no formal pastoral experience. Second, like my previous secular employers, they had to look beyond the physical and allow me the chance to utilize what I have on the inside. Even though we were there only three years, it was three very blessed years. Ben was born during our time there. We were blessed to make some cherished, lifelong friendships. These three years were tremendously educational in every respect. I learned to receive both praise and criticism in a constructive manner. I also learned to never assume that people really know what I can and cannot do. For example, at the end of our first month at Valley Head, we had a big dinner-on-the grounds Sunday. After I started enjoying my food, I happened to look up and noticed that numerous people were not eating but were watching me intently. I guess my notice of them startled them as much as it did me! To break the ice, one of the deacons reacted and said, "Brother Bryan, a lot of us didn't know you could feed yourself!" I burst out with laughter and said, "Brother, you don't get this fat and not know how to feed yourself!" All the spectators howled with laughter! From that moment, my first congregation and I really began to bond. My physical weaknesses had been used by God to facilitate three very blessed years.

During those three years, I witnessed weakness and strength emanate from the same source. This source was innocence and it came in the form of a child. Valley Head is set in a rural scene nestled at the head of two mountains. When we had Vacation Bible School (VBS), children came from all around including from the two mountains. During our first VBS, break time arose on the first day. Teachers lined up the students for the bathroom and while so doing, two of the children walked quietly outside. When a teacher retrieved them and asked what they were doing, they sincerely answered, "Going to the bushes". These two did not have the benefits of an indoor toilet at their home. The teacher politely showed them that our "bushes" were inside. These two children thought that was the grandest thing! From their raw innocence came forth the weakness of poverty and the strength of sincerity that humbled all of us who were attempting to minister to these youngsters. Instead they ministered to the VBS staff. Through these two, all of us learned anew to be grateful for all the vast amount of things we daily take for granted. Though impoverished, their sincerity and innocence reflected the purity of Jesus like no VBS program ever could. The event proved to be a much needed lesson in humility for us all, especially the pastor!

Another similar lesson was taught to all of us by a long-time resident of Valley Head. We all fondly referred to her as Ms. Willie. She lived on the side of the mountain just above Valley Head in a literal wooden and tar-paper shack. Offers were made to her over the years to provide better living arrangements but she would always gracefully decline the offers. Amazingly, she was as happy and content as any soul I have ever known regardless of income and/or economics. Our church and others honored her graceful declines but we always made sure she had plenty of food and firewood for her woodstove. Usually once a week, she would walk to town. Those blessed to cross her path were always met with her beautiful and warm greeting that poured forth from her humble soul. Her worldly poverty was vastly overshadowed by her inner wealth. Her love for and dependence upon the Lord kept her happy and content with whatever the Lord provided. These many years later, I will catch myself reflecting upon this saintly woman's heart. As I have more than once expressed frustrations over not knowing which cereal to buy among a hundred different brands or what cut of steak to take home and grill, I am humbled and challenged instead that I have the means to choose. Such means marred by my occasional frustrations shamefully pales in comparison with the God-ward content of Ms. Willie. Though weak in the eyes of the world, she forever stands as a tower of strength in my eyes and heart as well as in those of countless others who were blessed to know her.

Our three year tenure at Valley Head was short but sweet indeed. Renee was blessed with the opportunity to attend graduate school at the University of Alabama. Thus, we moved to Tuscaloosa in September of 1988. Thankfully, our wait for another pastorate was soon met the following month. Cornelius Chapel Baptist Church (CCBC) is a rural country church in western Tuscaloosa County. The town is called "Buhl", pronounced like "mule" only with a "b" instead of an "m". The souls that comprised this church were the salt of the earth. Early on, their theme was shared with me and it simply stated: "We are the church for folks that no other church wants". Now in the eyes of the church at large, this may have seemed to set CCBC up as being a weak church from the start. In the eyes of some other churches, we were looked down upon. Indeed, we accepted with open arms and hearts any and all that would come. The main emphasis of CCBC was outreach to children and youth. We had a bus and two vans used to pick them up and take them home. Of course, adults were welcomed to ride too. Many would consider what we did as a grandiose baby-sitting service. Such commentators did not share the heart of those who consistently poured their hearts and energies into reaching the young people.

Most of the youngsters came from low-income homes. Many of these homes had varying degrees of dysfunction. Alcohol was often the culprit. Nevertheless, as we taught and shared the love of

Christ with these youngsters, I personally witnessed a transformation more than once. For example, children were often neglected and abused. We would minister to them by providing good food, clothing and even basic hygiene measures. When allowed, such ministry was extended to the adults of these homes. The aforementioned transformation was most notable in the form of the prayers these youngsters would offer up for their parents and guardians. During altar calls, these youngsters would often come (on their own) to pray. It seemed the dirtiest, weakest and most neglected among them would pray with a degree of fervency and sincerity that could only come from a broken-hearted child. I would be silenced as I knelt beside them at the altar. I could not speak a prayer. My heart broke with them. I was humbled at the depth and sincerity of their prayers. They often prayed lovingly and longingly for their families. Sometimes, I found myself ashamed because the very ones for which these children prayed for out of love were often the victims of my scorn for their mistreatment and neglect of these precious ones. Therein, the epitomized weaknesses of neglected children met what should have been the stronger heart of their pastor; yet at those times, they ministered to me instead. They taught me about a Jesus-rooted love that was not weighed down by pre-conceived notions. When these youngsters prayed, I am convinced all the legions of heavenly angels stood at attention awaiting the Lord's command to respond as He so directed. Frankly though, I am sure that Jesus instead chose to deal personally with such as these. From time to time, I am blessed these twenty years later to meet up with these now grown children.

I will not mention their names but some of them have indeed undergone a transformation that only God can facilitate and provide. They are living lives that have risen above their unfortunate upbringings. They still pray. They are God's strength shown forth through weaknesses. They are living testaments that with God, all things are possible.

These children often drove me to do things that I never thought I or any other pastor would do. Soon after arriving at CCBC, I learned that the highlight of the church year was Vacation Bible School (VBS). The previous pastor was known to set a numeric goal for VBS attendance. If that goal was reached, he would swallow a live goldfish. I instead offered a different incentive. I vowed to fill my wooden leg with grape cool-aide and drink it if the goal was met. That first VBS, I set what I thought would be an unobtainable goal of 150. Those kids and workers excelled by reaching a peak number of 180! I will never drink grape cool-aide again! Other VBS goals of following years were also met and I found myself receiving pies in my face as well as being doused in a "dunkin" booth!

My weakness surrounding my wooden leg and physical differences proved to be an unexpected outreach tool. Most children served by CCBC had never seen or even heard of a wooden leg much less the likes of my hands! I soon learned to make it a habit to be in my pulpit chair when the bus and vans arrived. The kids would head straight for me. The boldest ones would roll up my left pants leg so the newcomers could see my "pine tree leg"! Others would hold and examine my hands All of this of course was accompanied by a barrage of questions all of which provided opportunities to share Jesus!

Herein is found one of the main reasons behind one of my most misunderstood declarations that says, "I wouldn't trade this body for the most perfect, physically normal body imaginable." Because of the combined weaknesses of my physical frame and its design, innumerable doors have been opened to share the Gospel. This has remained the case well after my tenure at CCBC ended. The youngsters there liberated me to be open and even candidly forward about my weaknesses and differences. Even though these youngsters were mostly weak, frail and poor in the eyes of the world, they instead proved to be for me an eternal elixir that had emboldened me as nothing else ever could. For this, I am eternally grateful to them and above all to Jesus. In a portion of Matthew 21:16, Jesus said it best: "…out of the mouth of babes and sucklings thou hast perfected praise…"(KJV).

My third and most recent pastorate was at Akron Baptist Church (ABC) in Akron, Alabama. Akron is a small, village-type town adjacent to a river busy with both industrial and recreational watercraft. As is the case with many rural towns in Alabama, Akron was once a stop for the railroad. Once that entity ended, the pace and vitality of the town changed dramatically. However, the people there are rooted in the principles of family, church and God and in so being, they prove to be survivors. The congregation at ABC is graced with the attributes that only southern charm can provide.

Their kindness and love are as pleasant as sweet potato pie! Their dedication to remaining a close-knit group was uniquely paired with the attribute of being an outreaching church to the needy. Their care for the tenants of the local veterans-care home was exemplary. Their love extended to families regardless of race and church affiliation. Their generosity to missions was far-reaching both locally and globally. I recall one young lady who was a non-member being presented a large sum of money that was instrumental in her serving one summer as a volunteer missionary in Africa. As their pastor, I will always readily admit that they pastored more to me than I to them. There were a number of personal, family trials that I experienced while at Akron including the extended illnesses and deaths of both my parents and my brother-in-law. All three lived three hours away. Not once did the folks at Akron ever exhibit anything but full support by allowing me to be there for my family. Like my first two churches, ABC blessed me with the opportunity to be their pastor despite my physical differences.

 ABC had a small group of children and an even smaller group of youth. Even though what we had to offer was sparse in the way of extra activities, they were faithful in coming through for special events like the Christmas play. During my ten and one-half years there, I was blessed to see a few of them reach adulthood. I was even privileged to perform some weddings among this group.

The adults at ABC definitely comprised the majority of the church. Most of these were senior citizens and many were relatives. I benefited greatly from the seasoned wisdom of this group. They taught me much about life and how to deal with the challenges of an aging body. Inevitably, I had the sad task of preaching several funerals throughout my time at Akron. Each of these passed loved ones had become a mentor to me in various ways. They nurtured me as I navigated the difficult waters of giving up my own family members. As a result, this small group of devoted Christians proved to be a catalyst in my launching this writing. When I resigned from being their pastor in order to devote time to writing this book, their support was second to none. Even though they made it quite clear that they did not want Renee and me to leave, they were resolute in my being obedient to the Lord's leadership. Their resolve strengthened me for this writing task as nothing else could. The deep bond between this precious group and me is one from which I will forever draw encouragement for the rest of my days no matter how challenging my physical weaknesses may prove to be. Of the folks at ABC, I echo the words of Paul in Philippians 1:3 that says, "I thank my God upon every remembrance of you." (KJV)

The Call of Pain: The Helping Hurt

The old adage that recommends walking a mile in the other fellow's shoes before judging him makes more sense with every passing day. I could fill volumes with examples of how I learned this lesson personally. To varying degrees, these lessons directly involve my physical weaknesses and the challenges they have posed. These lessons have left me bruised and battered at times but always in the end of the experience, I have been the better for it.

Dad always kept as upbeat as any man could with the load he toted. As mentioned earlier, my special needs undeniably caused financial strains but it was never mentioned by anyone. This fact became all too clear after I aged into the real world of paying my own bills! I remember from time to time how Dad would come home after a long, hard day and he would be irritable. My MaMa had the least tolerance for it and would ask him with exasperation, "Why are you so ill?!" I avoided the issue but always felt very bad for Dad. Once I was grown and dealing with the rigors of keeping a household afloat on a preacher's/teacher's salaries, I soon learned to be more sympathetic toward Dad. This was especially so the first time one of my sons asked me the same, exasperating question! Now, what does any of this have to do with weaknesses and God's involvement therein? Plenty! I always wanted to provide for my own the way Dad did for his. Scriptures declare that anyone who does not provide for his own is worse than an infidel (I Timothy 5:8, paraphrased from NKJV). As the years have passed, the amount of effort required to accomplish the tasks of the day are doubled. This is most frustrating to me and downright disconcerting at times. Even though I have simultaneously pastored and worked a secular employ for as long as I can remember, I always had in the back of my mind that I could do better with a "fit" body. Therein come the weaknesses. Satan loves to gouge and poke. I have always been the hardest on myself and Satan monopolizes on that in order to send me on a guilt trip. Only in recent years have I learned to counter this dilemma with the necessity of trusting deeper in the Lord. In Him, I lack nothing. My independent nature has had to adjust to a greater dependence upon Him. Despite Satan's lies, this adjustment is no sign of weakness because I know that I am becoming more spiritually fit in the process. It is a grand trade, really…less of me and more of Jesus. Though I grow a bit weaker and less mobile every year, the Lord's faithful provisions and grace shine through ever brighter in His response to my weaknesses. I, the weak thing in the hand of God, am still usable as long as I stay firmly in His grasp. That old hymn that challenges us to "hold to God's unchanging hand" is so precious to me. As long as I focus on Him and not on me, then truly I am made strong, though I am weak (taught in II Corinthians 12:10b).

In a previous chapter, I elaborated upon my Mother's physical and emotional challenges. Physically and emotionally, MaMa's pains were deep and challenging. I vividly recall as early as my college days that her osteoporosis, spinal curvature, and disintegrating bone mass presented a painful, daily obstacle. At that point in time, she would only give a general comment or two most days pertaining to her pain. Other days were more extenuating as proven by her tears that I witnessed more than once while she kept going with her homemaking chores. Admittedly, I did not understand the mental havoc that physical pain can wreak upon a person. When the first mention was made of securing psychiatric help to assist MaMa with her struggles, I protested. I thought she just needed to toughen up. I scorned the services of anything pertaining to psychological or psychiatric care. Despite my own pain, I did not understand. Oh how I wish I could go back and be more supportive of MaMa in her dilemma. Had I been so, I am convinced that she may have had an easier go of things when I left home. Only in the last several years have I learned to be sympathetic in regards to MaMa and others in need of mental counsel. I witnessed its benefits for her in her last few years of life when her body was so weak, feeble and pain-ridden. Even though I have never felt the need to seek such care for myself, I am open to the possibility as life and my pain levels progress. In fact, if utilizing strong measures of my mind and will can be a means by which I can forgo pain medications, then so be it! I have long been a staunch advocate of non-medicinal pain management…at least for myself. I am more than willing to administer medicinal measures for my family if they are in pain. Yes, I need to practice what I preach! Therein lurks a weakness of mine that I must submit to God's omnipotence. I place an uncanny emphasis upon maintaining clarity of mind, so much so that I will choose a high level of pain before I choose the painkiller. Unfortunately, this method can prove foolish if the pain is so severe that it impairs my thought processes. Patiently, fervently and at times through others, God shows me that it is no degradation of my manhood to take a Tylenol if needed. I know this sounds ridiculous to many but just as I have made adjustments by connecting with the pains of my MaMa and others, so too I implore the understanding of others who do not experience daily pain opposed to occasional discomfort.

Sympathizing is a two-way street. As my own experiences with pains and their accompanying weaknesses increase, I personally relate more and more to MaMa and others who have endured like her. In so doing, the Lord makes me stronger to assist others who hurt and this is a far cry better than the way than I used to deal with such! I humbly leave this matter by readily admitting that the Lord is still teaching me. On those days that I complain the most, He lovingly reminds me that He understands because He hurt more than anyone at Calvary.

After over thirty-three years in the Gospel ministry, I long since lost count of the number of funerals I have dealt with to one extent or the other. In order to be of as much help as possible during such times, I was compelled to remain as composed and objective as possible. Following the death of my parents, all that changed. No longer do I consider it a problem if during a eulogy, I must pause to wipe a tear and regain my thoughts. I have learned that a broken heart is best met by another heart of like wear. The world became a very different place when my parents left it. In this experience, I personally learned just how earth-changing and life-shattering is the event of losing a loved one, specifically within my immediate family. Simultaneously, I learned anew the indescribable power of God's sustenance and strength. Such times are fertile grounds for developing an intimacy with God as no other times can afford. Therein, my personal pain has made me immensely better equipped to reach out to the bereaved. I have learned that it is ok to grieve with them. Scriptural truths that comfort us with the fact that death is merely a simple passage through a door to enter real living as God originally intended has become infinitely more than words with which to facilitate comfort. Instead, these truths bind up my broken heart into a useful instrument once again so that I may hopefully be of some help to others. As broken and as weak as I realized myself to be when my parents died, God uses it all to make me more useable in His hands during the midst of the grief of others. I am so thankful for His doing so.

Also throughout my years in the ministry, I have spent countless hours visiting the sick and their families. I consider myself privileged during each of these hours. I recall the blessings I experienced as a patient when someone would visit me in the hospital or during my convalescing at home. Despite my physical challenges, I have been hospitalized only three times since I was fourteen. Each hospitalization reminded me to stay sharp and vigilant in my hospital visitation efforts. Being the patient is an invaluable reminder of how important it is to be cared for and prayed with. It also reminds me to mind my bedside manners! I have witnessed visitors who go through a long oratory of their own physical afflictions at the expense of the poor patient who cannot escape! On the other extreme, I have seen visitors whose demeanor makes it obvious that their visit is strictly obligatory. Such is hardly comforting to a patient either! The lesson learned: if a visit is going to add to a patient's pain and misery, just send them a card or flowers or call them by phone. "Pain begets pain" certainly applies if a visitor's heart does not embrace the best interests of the patient. A visit motivated from the heart is much more likely to be construed as being from God's hand and thereby considered to be a blessed event if it is kept brief! Again, a little bit in the hands of God goes a long way!

Finally, the sermon moment lends itself to be either painful or blessed. I reflect back on what the congregations of my early years endured and I am painfully embarrassed! I thought a sermon was not seasoned or ready for delivery until I had it all written down word-for-word! Humbling and painful are the moments when I listen to one of those thirty year old cassette tapes! I thought I had it all together back then. Thankfully, there were enough patient souls on the other side of the pulpit who after enduring the pain, would truthfully evaluate my rants! Needless to say, I have made numerous and extensive changes to my sermon preparations and deliveries. I still have much to learn but one of my greatest means of mastering my lingering, pulpit weaknesses is by purposely listening to the inexperienced preacher boys of today! They either remind me of what I need to avoid while some of them humble me with their abilities that far exceed their years! The bottom line to all of this: prayerfully prepare for the preaching moment. Being prepared greatly increases the chances that the hearts of the hearers will be touched, in addition to their eardrums! All of life's experiences are either embraced or denied from the pulpit. Their embracement incorporates the authenticity in the speaker that I am convinced is necessary to make a sermon purposeful and helpful in meeting the needs of the people. That is the reason why so often my pains and weaknesses are conveyed from the pulpit. I purposely avoid allowing either from overshadowing the Scriptures. Instead, Scriptures are best for showing how we can live out the fullest potentials of our pains and weaknesses rather than allowing these to become a constant, looming cloud of gloom and doom. I am thankful that the Lord has thereby utilized my weaknesses and pains for the highest purpose: His own. To God be the glory!

When God and Weakness Merge: Jesus

There is no match for the love, grace and power of the Almighty God. Yet, His epitomized expression of these three attributes is exhibited through the frailty of the human flesh---Jesus Christ---God Incarnate. In the fifty-third chapter of his prophecy, Isaiah details it as follows:

Isaiah 53:1-12 (KJV):

> [1] "Who hath believed our report? And to who is the arm of the Lord revealed? [2] For he shall grow up before him as a tender plant, and as root out of a dry ground; he hath no form or comeliness; and when we shall see him, there is no beauty that we should desire him. [3] He is despised and rejected of men; a man of sorrows, and acquainted with grief; and we hid as it were our faces from him,; he was despised and we esteemed him not. [4] Surely he hath borne our griefs, and carried our sorrows: yet we did not esteem him stricken, smitten of God, and afflicted. [5] But he was wounded for our transgressions, he was bruised for our iniquities; the chastisement of our peace was upon him; and with his stripes, we are healed. [6] All we like sheep have gone astray; we have turned everyone to his own way; and the LORD hath laid on him the iniquity of us all. [7] He was oppressed and he

was afflicted, yet, he opened not his mouth; he is brought as a lamb to the slaughter, and as a sheep before her shearers is dumb, so he openeth not his mouth [8] He was taken from prison and from judgment: and who shall declare his generation? For he was cut off out of the land of the living: for the transgression of my people was he stricken. [9] And he made his grace with the wicked, and with the rich in his death; because he had done no violence, neither was any deceit in his mouth. [10] Yet, it pleased the LORD to bruise him; he hath put him to grief: when thou shalt make his soul an offering for sin, he shall see his seed, he shall prolong his days, and the pleasure of the LORD shall prosper in his hand. [11] He shall see of the travail of his soul, and he shall be satisfied: by his knowledge shall my righteous servant justify many; for he shall bear their iniquities. [12] Therefore, I will divide him a portion with the great, and he shall divide the spoil with the strong; because he has poured out his soul unto death: and he was numbered with the transgressors; and he bare the sins of many, and made intercession for the transgressors."

Reader, please understand that even though I embrace Biblical inerrancy and Biblical authority, I by no means claim to be an exegetical expert and therefore, the following discussion of the cited passage is not offered as an exhaustive analysis thereof. Instead, I seek to use the truths therein to illustrate the very theme of this book. Under the directive of the Triune God, Jesus the Son left the portals of glory to accomplish what could not be accomplished in any other way and that is to overcome the chasm that sin caused between God and man. The love, power and grace displayed by God in so doing infinitely exceeds all other examples of the same combined. Another way of stating this matter is as follows:

Does God show forth Himself in a greater way through Jesus than He does through the following:

> -the creation process itself? (Genesis Chapters 1 & 2), or
>
> -through the parting of the Red Sea? (Exodus 14: 13-31), or
>
> -by stopping time to facilitate a military victory for His own? (Joshua 10:12-14), or
>
> -by teaching man through a talking donkey or a hungry, large fish? (Numbers 22:22-35, The Book of Jonah), or
>
> -through the defeat of a giant at the hands of a teenaged, shepherd boy? (I Samuel 17), or
>
> - through any of the New Testament miracles?, or
>
> -through Pentecost itself? (The Book of Acts)

In response to each of these, I offer a resounding "YES" and He does so by choosing to adopt the frail frame of humanity and therein, touches each of us with real, work-day power in the midst of our own, grappling weaknesses. Indeed, God could have remained in His due, lofty position on His throne and reached down to touch us from on high when He deemed fit. However, through the experience of Jesus (the Incarnate God), God ever-lovingly touches us in the midst of our struggles, cares and weaknesses and declares His ever-ready and sufficient, able help for us because He truly has "been there, done that" (albeit, without sin). Glory to His name! He totally and completely understands what we endure and encounter. With Jesus as our ever-present intercessor, God constantly stands mercifully ready to dispense to us whatever it takes for us to experience victory even if the entire world declares our defeat!

To the worldly ear, this all sounds so unbelievable. Isaiah relates that in the first of the cited chapter. Today as then, the world seeks some powerhouse figure of a hero to arrive and sweep away our agonies. Yet, Isaiah foretells of a coming Savior likened unto something as rare, frail, unassuming and unattractive as a tender piece of wild foliage shooting forth out of a desert ground. A weary, desert traveler would not likely give such a sight hardly any notice at all. They would probably figure: "That ugly weed will be dead in short order"!

A similar surmise was offered by the majority when Jesus arrived. A baby born into poverty, wrapped in rags, sleeping in a feed box frequented by hungry, slobbering, smelly cattle certainly did not fit the world's carnal expectation of a Savior King. Indeed, there were precious few that desired Him, that is, until He arose from the grave and ascended back to glory! The Book of Acts records the world's exploding attraction toward Him from that point! Prior to

His reveille, Isaiah 53:3 expounds upon the despicability with which the masses equated to Him. Man's rejection of Him was replete. The eventual sorrow and grief of His earthly end was so horrid that the world would not even look upon Him and thereby, totally discredited Him. Verse four reveals that He became so in order to spare us the same plight. Little did the masses know that as they rejected Him in His final hour, they did so because He took upon Himself the reprehensible vulgarity of us all—and they could not stand the sight of Him. Were it not for His doing this deed for us, God would have never stood for the equally deplorable sight that we all provide in the light of His perfect, just and holy sight.

Verse five explains that Jesus took upon Himself all that makes us total, eternal rejects as far as God is concerned. In so doing, we are (healed) made beautiful and fully desirous in God's eyes. Verse six reveals that our waywardness was redirected straight back to God because the total load of the lost and roaming was heaped upon Jesus.

Even though He sinned not, verse seven exhorts the blessed fact that not once did Jesus utter a word in His own defense. He assumed the pitiful, helpless role of the sacrificial lamb who could only wait to be stripped of all dignity and then of life itself. Yet, Scriptures teach that even in the midst of all this vile, helpless weakness, it was Jesus Himself who yielded up His life willingly when all else was finished!

Verse eight paints the picture of utter rejection. Despite His impeccability, Jesus was driven out of His own creation, totally rejected. Many things on earth are equated with rejection. A junk yard full of wrecked and worn out cars tell the fickle story of humanity. Even though those cars were once brand new and their owner's pride, they now are scorned, ignored and rejected. I once viewed a television documentary about the poultry industry. New hatchlings go through a culling process. The rejects meet a horrid fate that I will not describe here. Infinitely worse still are the countless number of unborn humans torn from their mother's wombs, rejected, unwanted and discarded. Equally despicable is the treatment to the newborns found in trash dumpsters and public toilets. Their fate of rejection equals that of refuse and dung. Like Jesus, they are "cut out of the land of the living". Verse eight portrays weakness in its most vivid form…the rejection of innocence. Thus, grievous, stricken humanity was spared as Jesus Himself took upon Himself all that would cause us to be rejected by God.

Verse nine expounds upon the humiliating criminal's death Jesus endured. Had it not been for Joseph of Arimathaea, His remains could have very well met the same common fate of executed criminals of that day by being thrown into an exiled heap to rot and be eaten by wild animals. Yet, the very source of life itself was placed lifeless in a grave. But alas, the last three verses of Isaiah Chapter 53 explode with the news of immeasurable strength to come forth from such total weakness!

From the sacrifice of Jesus comes an eternity of new life for countless numbers ("He shall see His seed", v.10) who will abide with Him throughout a prolonging of days which has no end to their joy and prosperity! His sacrifice procures God's total satisfaction that the price of sin is paid in full, thereby freely providing us justification (verses 11-12). The prize afforded to us is referred to by the Apostle Paul as being "unsearchable riches" (Ephesians 3:8 KJV) yet it comes to us via the throes of the lowliest weaknesses. Jesus Christ, God Incarnate, willingly, purposely, and with full sovereignty reduced Himself to the weakest of all forms that was so vile with our sin that God the Heavenly Father would not even look upon Him. In so doing, Jesus removes the eternal punishment for sin from us to Himself so that God beholds those who receive Christ, He sees that which He loves immeasurably---His own---justified from all sin that has been cast into the "depths of the sea" (Micah 7:19 KJV). No amount of praise unto Him is enough! All of this was done for humanity so that each of us can be made and transformed from sinful wretches, who are helplessly weak in our sin, to heirs of the King of Kings and Lord of Lords.

In so doing, the weak things in God's hands are thereby made eternally and gloriously strong! May His sweet Name be forever praised for the great things He has done! Amen

www.ingramcontent.com/pod-product-compliance
Lightning Source LLC
Chambersburg PA
CBHW052108110526
44592CB00013B/1531